Chicken

Everyday Cookery

STAR
FIRE

This is a Starfire book
First published in 2005

05 07 09 08 06

1 3 5 7 9 10 8 6 4 2

Starfire is part of
The Foundry Creative Media Company Limited
Crabtree Hall, Crabtree Lane, Fulham, London, SW6 6TY

Visit our website: www.star-fire.co.uk

ISBN: 1-84451-315-7

The CIP record for this book is available from the British Library.

Printed in China

ACKNOWLEDGEMENTS

Publisher and Creative Director: Nick Wells
Project Editor and Editorial: Sarah Goulding
Design and Production: Chris Herbert, Mike Spender, Colin Rudderham and Claire Walker

Authors: Catherine Atkinson, Juliet Barker, Gina Steer, Vicki Smallwood,
Carol Tennant, Mari Mererid Williams, Elizabeth Wolf-Cohen and Simone Wright
Editorial: Gina Steer and Karen Fitzpatrick
Photography: Colin Bowling, Paul Forrester and Stephen Brayne
Home Economists and Stylists: Jacqueline Bellefontaine,
Mandy Phipps, Vicki Smallwood and Penny Stephens

All props supplied by Barbara Stewart at Surfaces

NOTE
Recipes using uncooked eggs should be avoided by infants,
the elderly, pregnant women and anyone suffering from an illness.

Contents

Exotic Recipes

Eastern Recipes

Quick Recipes

Hygiene in the Kitchen

It is important to remember that many foods can carry some form of bacteria. In most cases, the worst it will lead to is a bout of food poisoning or gastroenteritis, although for certain people this can be serious. The risk can be reduced or eliminated, however, by good hygiene and proper cooking.

Do not buy food that is past its sell-by date and do not consume food that is past its use-by date. When buying food, use the eyes and nose. If the food looks tired, limp or a bad colour or it has a rank, acrid or simply bad smell, do not buy or eat it under any circumstances.

Take special care when preparing raw meat and fish. A separate chopping board should be used for each, and the knife, board and your hands should be thoroughly washed before handling or preparing any other food.

Regularly clean, defrost and clear out the refrigerator or freezer – it is worth checking the packaging to see exactly how long each product is safe to freeze. Avoid handling food if suffering from an upset stomach as bacteria can be passed on through food preparation.

Dish cloths and tea towels must be washed and changed regularly. Ideally use disposable cloths which should be replaced on a daily basis. More durable cloths should be left to soak in bleach, then washed in the washing machine at a high temperature.

Keep your hands, cooking utensils and food preparation surfaces clean and do not allow pets to climb on to any work surfaces.

Buying

Avoid bulk buying where possible, especially fresh produce such as meat, poultry, fish, fruit and vegetables. Fresh foods lose their nutritional value rapidly, so buying a little at a time minimises loss of nutrients. It also means your fridge won't be so full, which reduces the effectiveness of the refrigeration process.

When buying prepackaged goods such as cans or pots of cream and yogurts, check that the packaging is intact and not damaged or pierced at all. Cans should not be dented, pierced or rusty. Check the sell-by dates even for cans and packets of dry ingredients such as flour and rice. Store fresh foods in the refrigerator as soon as possible – not in the car or the office.

When buying frozen foods, ensure that they are not heavily iced on the outside and that the contents feel completely frozen. Ensure that the frozen foods have been stored in the cabinet at the correct storage level and the temperature is below -18°C/ -0.4°F. Pack in cool bags to transport home and place in the freezer as soon as possible after purchase.

Preparation

Make sure that all work surfaces and utensils are clean and dry. Hygiene should be given priority at all times. Separate chopping boards should be used for raw and cooked meats, fish and vegetables. Currently, a variety of good quality plastic boards come in various designs and colours. This makes differentiating easier and the plastic has the added hygienic advantage of being washable at high temperatures in the dishwasher. If using the board for fish, first wash in cold water, then in hot to prevent odour. Also remember that knives and utensils should always be thoroughly cleaned after use.

When cooking, be particularly careful to keep cooked and raw food separate to avoid any contamination. It is worth washing all fruits and vegetables regardless of whether they are going to be eaten raw or lightly cooked. This rule should apply even to prewashed herbs and salads.

Do not reheat food more than once. If using a microwave, always check that the food is piping hot all the way through – in theory, the food should reach 70°C/158°F and needs to be cooked at that temperature for at least three minutes to ensure that all bacteria are killed.

All poultry must be thoroughly thawed before using, including chicken and poussin. Remove the food to be thawed from the freezer and place in a shallow dish to contain the juices. Leave the food in the refrigerator until it is completely thawed. A 1.4 kg/3 lb whole chicken will take about 26–30 hours to thaw. To speed up the process, immerse the chicken in cold water, making sure that the water is changed regularly. When the joints can move freely and no ice crystals remain in the cavity, the bird is completely thawed.

Once thawed, remove the wrapper and pat the chicken dry. Place the chicken in a shallow dish, cover lightly and store as close to the base of the refrigerator as possible. The chicken should be cooked as soon as possible. Some foods can be cooked from

frozen including many prepacked foods such as soups, sauces, casseroles and breads. Where applicable follow the manufacturers' instructions.

Vegetables and fruits can also be cooked from frozen, but meats and fish should be thawed first. The only time food can be refrozen is when the food has been thoroughly thawed then cooked. Once the food has cooled then it can be frozen again, but it should only be stored for one month.

All poultry and game (except for duck) must be cooked thoroughly. When cooked, the juices will run clear on the thickest part of the bird – the best area to try is usually the thigh. Other meats, like minced meat and pork should be cooked right the way through. Fish should turn opaque, be firm in texture and break easily into large flakes.

When cooking leftovers, make sure they are reheated until piping hot and that any sauce or soup reaches boiling point first.

Storing, Refrigerating and Freezing

Meat, poultry, fish, seafood and dairy products should all be refrigerated. The temperature of the refrigerator should be between 1–5°C/34–41°F while the freezer temperature should not rise above -18°C/-0.4°F.

To ensure the optimum refrigerator and freezer temperature, avoid leaving the door open for long periods of time. Try not to overstock the refrigerator as this reduces the airflow inside and therefore the effectiveness in cooling the food within.

When refrigerating cooked food, allow it to cool down quickly and completely before refrigerating. Hot food will raise the temperature of the refrigerator and possibly affect or spoil other food stored in it.

Food within the refrigerator and freezer should always be covered. Raw and cooked food should be stored in separate parts of the refrigerator. Cooked food should be kept on the top shelves of the refrigerator, while raw meat, poultry and fish should be placed on bottom shelves to avoid

drips and cross-contamination. It is recommended that eggs should be refrigerated in order to maintain their freshness and shelf life.

Take care that frozen foods are not stored in the freezer for too long. Blanched vegetables can be stored for one month; beef, lamb, poultry and pork for six months and unblanched vegetables and fruits in syrup for a year. Oily fish and sausages should be stored for three months. Dairy products can last four to six months, while cakes and pastries should be kept in the freezer for three to six months.

High Risk Foods

Certain foods may carry risks to people who are considered vulnerable such as the elderly, the ill, pregnant women, babies, young infants and those suffering from a recurring illness.

It is advisable to avoid those foods listed below which belong to a higher-risk category.

There is a slight chance that some eggs carry the bacteria salmonella. Cook the eggs until both the yolk and the white are firm to eliminate this risk. Pay particular attention to dishes and products incorporating lightly cooked or raw eggs which should be eliminated from the diet. Hollandaise sauce, mayonnaise, mousses, soufflés and meringues all use raw or lightly cooked eggs, as do custard-based dishes, ice creams and sorbets. These are all considered high-risk foods to the vulnerable groups mentioned above.

Certain meats and poultry also carry the potential risk of salmonella and so should be cooked thoroughly

until the juices run clear and there is no pinkness left. Unpasteurised products such as milk, cheese (especially soft cheese), pâté, meat (both raw and cooked) all have the potential risk of listeria and should be avoided.

When buying seafood, buy from a reputable source which has a high turnover to ensure freshness. Fish should have bright clear eyes, shiny skin and bright pink or red gills. The fish should feel stiff to the touch, with a slight smell of sea air and iodine. The flesh of fish steaks and fillets should be translucent with no signs of discolouration. Molluscs such as scallops, clams and mussels are sold fresh and are still alive. Avoid any that are open or do not close when tapped lightly. In the same way, univalves such as cockles or winkles should withdraw back into their shells when lightly prodded. When choosing cephalopods such as squid and octopus they should have a firm flesh and pleasant sea smell.

As with all fish, whether it is shellfish or seafish, care is required when freezing it. It is imperative to check whether the fish has been frozen before. If it has been frozen, then it should not be frozen again under any circumstances.

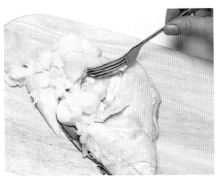

Nutrition The Role of Essential Nutrients

A healthy and well-balanced diet is the body's primary energy source. In children, it constitutes the building blocks for future health as well as providing lots of energy. In adults, it encourages self-healing and regeneration within the body. A well-balanced diet will provide the body with all the essential nutrients it needs. This can be achieved by eating a variety of foods, demonstrated in the pyramid below.

FATS

PROTEINS

milk,	meat, fish,
yogurt	poultry, eggs,
and cheese	nuts and pulses

FRUITS AND VEGETABLES

STARCHY CARBOHYDRATES
cereals, potatoes, bread, rice and pasta

FATS

Fats fall into two categories: saturated and unsaturated. It is very important that a healthy balance is achieved within the diet. Fats are an essential part of the diet: they are a source of energy and provide essential fatty acids and fat soluble vitamins. The right balance of fats should boost the body's immunity to infection and keep muscles, nerves and arteries in good condition. Saturated fats are of animal origin and are hard when stored at room temperature. They can be found in dairy produce, meat, eggs, margarines and hard white cooking fat (lard) as well as in manufactured products such as pies, biscuits and cakes. A high intake of saturated fat over many years has been proven to increase heart disease and high blood cholesterol levels and often leads to weight gain. The aim of a healthy diet is to keep the fat content low in the foods that we eat. Lowering the amount of saturated fat that we consume is very important, but this does not mean that it is good to consume lots of other types of fat.

There are two kinds of unsaturated fats: polyunsaturated and monounsaturated. Polyunsaturated fats include safflower, soybean, corn and sesame oils. Within the polyunsaturated group are Omega oils. The Omega-3 oils are of significant interest because they have been found to be particularly beneficial to coronary health and can encourage brain growth and development. Omega-3 oils are derived from oily fish such as salmon, mackerel, herring, pilchards and sardines. It is recommended that we should eat these types of fish at least once a week. However, for those who do not eat fish or who are vegetarians, liver oil supplements are available in most supermarkets and health shops. It is suggested that these supplements should be taken on a daily basis. The most popular oils that are high in monounsaturates are olive oil, sunflower oil and peanut oil. The Mediterranean diet which is based on a diet high in monounsaturated fats is recommended for heart health. Monounsaturated fats are also known to help reduce the levels of cholestrol.

PROTEINS

Composed of amino acids – proteins' building blocks – proteins perform a wide variety of essential functions for the body, including supplying energy and building and repairing tissues. Good sources of proteins are eggs, milk, yogurt, cheese, meat, fish, poultry, eggs, nuts and pulses. (See the second level of the pyramid.) Some of these foods, however, contain saturated fats. To strike a nutritional balance, eat generous amounts of vegetable protein foods such as soya, beans, lentils, peas and nuts.

FRUITS AND VEGETABLES

N ot only are fruits and vegetables the most visually appealing foods, but they are extremely good for us, providing essential vitamins and minerals essential for growth, repair and protection in the human body. Fruits and vegetables are low in calories and are responsible for regulating the body's metabolic processes and controlling the composition of its fluids and cells.

MINERALS

CALCIUM Important for healthy bones and teeth, nerve transmission, muscle contraction, blood clotting and hormone function. Calcium promotes a healthy heart, improves skin, relieves aching muscles and bones, maintains the correct acid-alkaline balance and reduces menstrual cramps. Good sources are dairy products, the bones of small fish, nuts, pulses, fortified white flours, breads and green leafy vegetables.

CHROMIUM Part of the glucose tolerance factor, chromium balances blood sugar levels, helps to normalise hunger and reduce cravings, improves lifespan, helps protect DNA and is essential for heart function. Good sources are brewer's yeast, wholemeal bread, rye bread, oysters, potatoes, green peppers, butter and parsnips.

IODINE Important for the manufacture of thyroid hormones and for normal development. Good sources of iodine are seafood, seaweed, milk and dairy products.

IRON As a component of haemoglobin, iron carries oxygen around the body. It is vital for normal growth and development. Good sources are liver, corned beef, red meat, fortified breakfast cereals, pulses, green leafy vegetables, egg yolk, cocoa and cocoa products.

MAGNESIUM Important for efficient functioning of metabolic enzymes and development of the skeleton. Magnesium promotes healthy muscles by helping them to relax and is therefore good for PMS. It is also important for heart muscles and the nervous system. Good sources are nuts, green vegetables, meat, cereals, milk and yogurt.

PHOSPHORUS Forms and maintains bones and teeth, builds muscle tissue, helps maintain pH of the body and aids metabolism and energy production. Phosphorus is present in almost all foods.

POTASSIUM Enables nutrients to move into cells while waste products move out; promotes healthy nerves and muscles; maintains fluid balance in the body; helps secretion of insulin for blood sugar control to produce constant energy; relaxes muscles; maintains heart functioning and stimulates gut movement to encourage proper elimination. Good sources are fruit, vegetables, milk and bread.

SELENIUM Antioxidant properties help to protect against free radicals and carcinogens. Selenium reduces inflammation, stimulates the immune system to fight infections, promotes a healthy heart and helps vitamin E's action. It is also required for the male reproductive system and is needed for metabolism. Good sources are tuna, liver, kidney, meat, eggs, cereals, nuts and dairy products.

SODIUM Important in helping to control body fluid and balance, preventing dehydration. Sodium is involved in muscle and nerve function and helps move nutrients into cells. All foods are good sources. Processed, pickled and salted foods are richest in sodium but should be eaten in moderation.

ZINC Important for metabolism and the healing of wounds. It also aids ability to cope with stress, promotes a healthy nervous system and brain especially in the growing foetus, aids bone and teeth formation and is essential for constant energy. Good sources are liver, meat, pulses, wholegrain cereals, nuts and oysters.

VITAMINS

VITAMIN A Important for cell growth and developmemt and for the formation of visual pigments in the eye. Vitamin A comes in two forms: retinol and beta-carotenes. Retinol is found in liver, meat and meat products and whole milk and its products. Beta-carotene is a powerful antioxidant and is found in red and yellow fruits and vegetables such as carrots, mangoes and apricots.

VITAMIN B1 Important in releasing energy from carbohydrate-containing foods. Good sources are yeast and yeast products, bread, fortified breakfast cereals and potatoes.

VITAMIN B2 Important for metabolism of proteins, fats and carbohydrates to produce energy. Good sources are meat, yeast extracts, fortified breakfast cereals and milk and its products.

VITAMIN B3 Required for the metabolism of food into energy production. Good sources are milk and milk products, fortified breakfast cereals, pulses, meat, poultry and eggs.

VITAMIN B5 Important for the metabolism of food and energy production. All foods are good sources but especially fortified breakfast cereals, wholegrain bread and dairy products.

VITAMIN B6 Important for metabolism of protein and fat. Vitamin B6 may also be involved in the regulation of sex hormones. Good sources are liver, fish, pork, soya beans and peanuts.

VITAMIN B12 Important for the production of red blood cells and DNA. It is vital for growth and the nervous system. Good sources are meat, fish, eggs, poultry and milk.

BIOTIN Important for metabolism of fatty acids. Good sources of biotin are liver, kidney, eggs and nuts. Micro-organisms also manufacture this vitamin in the gut.

VITAMIN C Important for healing wounds and the formation of collagen which keeps skin and bones strong. It is an important antioxidant. Good sources are fruits, especially soft summer fruits, and vegetables.

VITAMIN D Important for absorption and handling of calcium to help build bone strength. Good sources are oily fish, eggs, whole milk and milk products, margarine and of course sufficient exposure to sunlight, as vitamin D is made in the skin.

VITAMIN E Important as an antioxidant vitamin helping to protect cell membranes from damage. Good sources are vegetable oils, margarines, seeds, nuts and green vegetables.

FOLIC ACID Critical during pregnancy for the development of the brain and nerves. It is always essential for brain and nerve function and is needed for utilising protein and red blood cell formation. Good sources are whole-grain cereals, fortified breakfast cereals, green leafy vegetables, oranges and liver.

VITAMIN K Important for controlling blood clotting. Good sources are cauliflower, Brussels sprouts, lettuce, cabbage, beans, broccoli, peas, asparagus, potatoes, corn oil, tomatoes and milk.

CARBOHYDRATES

C arbohydrates are an energy source and come in two forms: starch and sugar. Starch carbohydrates are also known as complex carbohydrates and they include all cereals, potatoes, breads, rice and pasta. (See the fourth level of the pyramid). Eating whole-grain varieties of these foods also provides fibre. Diets high in fibre are believed to be beneficial in helping to prevent bowel cancer and can also keep cholesterol down. High-fibre diets are also good for those concerned about weight gain. Fibre is bulky and fills the stomach, therefore reducing hunger pangs. Sugar carbohydrates which are also known as fast release carbohydrates because of the quick fix of energy they give to the body, and include sugar and sugar-sweetened products such as jams and syrups. Milk provides lactose which is a milk sugar and fruits provide fructose which is a fruit sugar.

Varieties of Potatoes and Storage

Potatoes are an important component of many of the recipes in this book. The humble potato is generally taken for granted and the versatility and huge number of varieties of this delicious vegetable are often forgotten. Worldwide there are thousands of different types of potato and for about two-thirds of the world, they are the staple food. In this country, almost three-quarters of main crop potatoes are made up of just five varieties. Consumers have gradually become more demanding, however, so a wider range of potatoes suitable for different uses is now available. Although you will still find bags simply labelled 'red' and 'white' in supermarkets, alongside them is also a selection of named varieties.

Potatoes are classified according to how early in the season they are ready for harvesting and are correspondingly named first early, second early and main crop. The first earlies are the first new potatoes on the market; they are very fresh and young and the skins can simply be rubbed off. The second earlies are still new potatoes, but their skins will have begun to set. These potatoes will be difficult to scrape and are better cooked in their skins. Main crop potatoes are available all year round and may have been stored for several months. Individual potato varieties have their own characteristics. Some main crop varieties are better for boiling than baking and vice versa, so choose the most appropriate type of potato for the dish being prepared.

Check the label, ask your retailer or refer to the list below for guidance.

Ailsa (main crop) These medium-sized potatoes are round or oval with white skins and creamy-coloured, floury flesh. Ailsa potatoes are excellent for boiling and chipping.

Anya (second early) These speciality, knobbly, oval-shaped potatoes have a pinkish skin and white flesh. They have a nutty flavour and waxy texture and are at their best when boiled or used in salads.

Arran Comet (first early) These round, and sometimes oval, new potatoes have a white skin and creamy flesh. Large ones are good for chipping.

Arran Pilot (first early) The firm flesh of these potatoes makes them an ideal choice for salads. They have white flesh and skins.

Arran Victory (main crop) These oval-shaped potatoes have a deep purple skin and a bright white flesh. They are the oldest variety of Arran potatoes still available. Arran Victory potatoes have a very floury texture and flavour and are excellent for baking and boiling. Currently they are undergoing a revival – it is well worth seeking this variety out.

Asperge (second early) Also known as la ratte and cornichon, these potatoes have a yellow skin and a creamy, very waxy flesh. They are good steamed or boiled and are perfect for salads.

Belle de Fontenay (early main crop) These long potatoes often have a curved shape. Their skins are pale yellow and their flesh is firm, waxy and yellow. They have a wonderful buttery flavour and are particularly good boiled, in salads or mashed.

Bintje (main crop) With a pale yellow skin and flesh, these potatoes are suitable for all cooking methods and make particularly good chips.

Cara (late main crop) These potatoes may be white or red, round or oval. The flesh is creamy-coloured with a mild flavour and waxy texture. Cara are good all-round potatoes.

Catriona (second early) Kidney-shaped potatoes with purple markings around the eyes on the skin and a pale yellow flesh. They have a delicious flavour and are ideal for baking, boiling and mashing.

Charlotte (main crop) Oval or pear-shaped potatoes with pale yellow skin and flesh, a firm, waxy texture and a flavour not unlike chestnuts. They are particulary good boiled, steamed and in salads but can also be baked.

Cleopatra (first early) These oval, new potatoes are suitable for boiling, have pink or red skin and a light-yellow, dense flesh.

Colmo (first early) Medium round or oval, these potatoes have a white skin and golden, firm flesh. Their texture and colour make them particularly good for mashing.

Desiree (main crop) Probably the world's most popular red-skinned potatoes with pale yellow flesh, a firm texture and good flavour. These potatoes are good all-rounders and are great for both mashing and roasting. They also hold their shape well enough for boiling.

Diamont (main crop) These potatoes were a common and popular variety in the 1930s and are still available now. They are long and oval shaped with a rough, white skin and a firm, waxy yellow interior. Their flavour is slightly sharp and nutty.

Duke of York (first early) These long, oval new potatoes have a sweet flavour, firm texture, pale creamy skins and light yellow flesh. A red-skinned variety is also available.

Epicure (first early) Round potatoes with white or sometimes pink-tinged skin, creamy, firm flesh and a distinctive flavour. Suitable for both boiling and baking.

Estima (second early) Oval-shaped potatoes with a light yellow skin and flesh. Their firm, moist texture and subtle flavour make them good baking potatoes. These potatoes were the first yellow-fleshed potatoes to become popular.

Golden Wonder (late main crop) These large, oval potatoes have a dark, russet-coloured skin and light yellow flesh. They are excellent for baking and their floury texture makes them especially good for crisps.

Home Guard (first early) Round or slightly oval, with white skins and creamy-coloured flesh, these potatoes have a dry, floury texture and a good flavour with slightly bitter overtones. These potatoes are ideal for boiling, roasting and chipping. They were a favourite during the Second World War and are one of the first varieties of new potatoes available.

Jersey Royals (second early) The best and most popular new potatoes, Jersey Royals have a creamy-coloured skin and flesh and can be served both hot or cold. When cooked (boiled or steamed), they are tender rather than firm and are best served whole, with or without the skins.

Kerr's Pink (late main crop) Round, pink-skinned potatoes with creamy-white flesh and a floury texture, these potatoes are suitable for boiling, baking, mashing, roasting and chipping.King Edward (main crop) These large white-skinned potatoes are among the best known and most popular. They have creamy-coloured, very floury flesh and are good all-rounders. They are particularly suited to roasting and baking, but are not so good for salads.

Marfona (second early) These are good baking potatoes, also suitable for boiling, but not for roasting.

Maris Bard (first early) These white-skinned potatoes have firm, waxy flesh with a slightly earthy taste. They are good for boiling and suitable for most other methods. They should be avoided late in the season, however, when they lose their flavour and are in danger of disintegrating during cooking.

Maris Peer (second early) These potatoes have white flesh and skins with an excellent flavour. They are good for salads as well as boiling and steaming.

Morag (main crop) These potatoes have a pale skin and a white, waxy flesh. Serve them boiled, steamed or baked.

Nadine (second early) These potatoes are available in two sizes. There are the small new potatoes and the slightly larger-sized potatoes which are suitable for baking. Nadine potatoes have creamy-yellow skins and white, waxy flesh, but their flavour is somewhat bland.

Pentland Javelin (first early) These new potatoes have very white, smooth skins and milky-white flesh. These potatoes are ideal for salads, but are also good boiled or steamed.

Pentland Squire (main crop) Usually white skinned, but occasionally russet, the flesh of these potatoes is very white. Their floury texture makes them perfect for baking. They are also good for boiling and mashing, but are poor in salads.

Pink Fir Apple (main crop) These knobbly, misshapen potatoes have white skins with a pinkish blush and a pale yellow flesh. They are firm and waxy with a delicious nutty flavour and have many of the characteristics of new potatoes. They are best cooked in their skins as their shape makes them extremely difficult to peel and are good steamed, boiled and served cold in salads.

Shelagh (main crop) This Scottish variety has a creamy flesh and pinkish patches all over the skin. The waxy texture of these potatoes makes them good for boiling, steaming or chipping.

Wilja (second early) These potatoes have pale yellow skins and flesh. They are good, flavoursome all-rounders and hold their shape when cooked, so are particularly suitable for salads, boiling and steaming. They can also be used for baking and roasting.

Sweet Potatoes These potatoes are imported from tropical areas of the Americas and from many other hot countries around the world. Their skins are red and the flesh inside is either white or orange. Orange-fleshed sweet potatoes have a denser, waxier texture and tend to hold their shape better, whereas white-fleshed ones are starchier and not quite as sugary. It is impossible to tell from the outside what colour the flesh will be within, so unless labelled you may need to scrape off a small patch of skin. Treat in much the same way as ordinary potatoes – bake, mash or fry.

Buying and Storage

When buying potatoes, always choose ones with smooth, firm skins. When purchasing new potatoes, check that they are really young and fresh by scraping the skin – it should peel away very easily. Only buy the quantity you need and use within a couple of days. Check main crop potatoes to make sure that they are firm and not sprouting or showing any signs of mould. Avoid buying and discard any potatoes with greenish patches or carefully cut them out. These parts of the potato are toxic and a sign that they have been stored in light.

Potatoes should be stored in a cool, dark place but not in the refrigerator as the dampness will make them sweat, causing mould to grow. If the potatoes come in plastic bags, take them out and store in a paper bag or on a vegetable rack. If you prefer to buy in bulk, keep the potatoes in a cold, dark, dry place such as a larder or garage, making sure that they do not freeze in cold weather.

Sweet potatoes should be stored in a cool, dry place, but unlike ordinary potatoes, do not need to be kept in the dark.

Cooking Techniques for Potatoes

Generally, new potato varieties have a firm and waxy texture that do not break up during cooking, so are ideal for boiling, steaming and salads. Main crop potatoes, on the other hand, have a more floury texture and lend themselves to mashing and roasting – both types are suitable for chips. When cooking potatoes, it is important to make sure the potatoes that you are using are the correct type for the dish being prepared. Whichever way you choose to serve potatoes, allow 175–225 g/6–8 oz per person.

Boiling Potatoes
New Potatoes

Most of the new potatoes available nowadays are fairly clean – especially those sold in supermarkets – and simply need a light scrub before cooking in their skins. If the potatoes are very dirty, use a small scrubbing brush or scourer to remove both the skins and dirt. Add them to a pan of cold, salted water and bring to the boil. Cover the pan with a lid and simmer for 12–15 minutes or until tender. Add a couple of sprigs of fresh herbs to the pan if you like – fresh mint is traditionally used to flavour potatoes. Drain the potatoes thoroughly and

serve hot, tossed in a little melted butter or, for a change, a tablespoon of pesto. The skins of first early new potatoes will peel away easily, but second earlies should be served in their skins or peeled when cooked – hold the hot potatoes with a fork to make this easier. Very firm new potatoes can be added to boiling water, simmered for 8 minutes, and then left to stand in the hot water for a further 10 minutes until cooked through.

Old Potatoes

Choose a main crop potato suitable for boiling, then thinly peel and cut into even-sized pieces. Add to a saucepan of cold, salted water and bring to the boil. Cover the pan with a lid and simmer for 20 minutes or until tender.

Alternatively, you can cook the potatoes in their skins and peel them after cooking. It is particularly important to cook floury potatoes gently or the outsides may start to fall apart before they are tender in the centre. Drain the potatoes in a colander, then return them to the pan to dry out over a very low heat for 1–2 minutes. If you are planning to serve the potatoes mashed, roughly mash them and add a knob of butter and

2 tablespoons of milk per person. Mash until smooth, either with a hand masher, mouli grater or a potato ricer. Season to taste with salt, freshly ground black pepper and a little freshly grated nutmeg if liked, then beat for a few seconds with a wooden spoon until fluffy. As an alternative to butter, use a good quality olive oil or crème fraîche. Finely chopped red and green chillies, crispy-cooked crumbled bacon, fresh herbs or grated Parmesan cheese can also be stirred in for additional flavour.

Steaming Potatoes

All potatoes are suitable for steaming. Floury potatoes, however, are ideal for this method of cooking as they fall apart easily.

New and small potatoes can be steamed whole, but larger ones should be cut into even-sized pieces. Place the potatoes in a steamer, colander or sieve over boiling water and cover. Steam for 10 minutes if the potatoes are very small or if they are cut into large chunks cook for 20–25 minutes.

Frying Potatoes
Chipped Potatoes

To make chips, wash, peel and cut the potatoes into 1.5 cm/½ inch slices. Cut the slices into long strips also about 1.5 cm/½ inch wide. Place the strips in a bowl of cold water and leave for 20 minutes, then drain and dry well on kitchen paper – moisture will make the fat spit. Pour some oil into a deep, heavy-based saucepan or deep-fat fryer, making sure that the oil does not go any further than halfway up the sides of the pan. Heat the oil to 190°C/375°F, or until a chip dropped into the fat rises to the surface straight away and is surrounded by bubbles. Put the chips into a wire basket and lower into the oil and cook for 7–8 minutes or until golden. Remove and increase the heat of the oil to 200°C/400°F. Lower the chips into the oil again and cook for 2–3 minutes, or until they are crisp and golden brown. Drain on kitchen paper before serving.

Slightly finer chips are properly known as *pommes frites*, even finer ones as *pommes allumettes* and the finest of all as *pommes pailles* (straw chips). Paper-thin slices of peeled potatoes, cut with a sharp knife or using a mandoline or food processor, can be deep-fried a few at a time to make crisps or game chips.

Healthy Chips

To make lower-fat chips, preheat the oven to 200°C/400°F/Gas Mark 6 and place a non-stick baking tray in the oven to heat up. Cut the potatoes into chips as above or into chunky wedges, if preferred. Put the chips or wedges in a pan of cold water and quickly bring to the boil. Simmer for 2 minutes, then drain in a colander. Leave for a few minutes to dry, then drizzle over 1½–2 tablespoons of olive or sunflower oil and toss to coat. Tip on to the heated baking tray and cook in the preheated oven for 20–25 minutes, turning occasionally until golden brown and crisp.

Sauteed Potatoes

Cut peeled potatoes into rounds about 0.5 cm/¼ inch thick and pat dry. Heat 25 g/1 oz unsalted butter and 2 tablespoons of oil in a large, heavy-based frying pan until hot. Add the potatoes in a single layer and cook for 4–5 minutes until the undersides are golden. Turn with a large fish slice and cook the other side until golden and tender. Drain on kitchen paper and sprinkle with a little salt before serving.

Baking Potatoes

Allow a 300–350 g/11–12 oz potato per person and choose a variety such as Maris Piper, Cara or King Edward. Wash and dry the potatoes, prick the skins lightly, then rub each one with a little oil and sprinkle with salt. Bake at 200°C/400°F/Gas Mark 6 for 1–1½ hours or until the skins are

crisp and the centres are very soft. To speed up the cooking time, thread on to metal skewers as this conducts heat to the middle of the potatoes.

Roasting Potatoes

For crisp and brown outsides and fluffy centres choose potatoes suitable for baking. Thinly peel the potatoes and cut into even-sized pieces. Drop them into a pan of boiling, salted water and simmer for 5 minutes. Turn off the heat and leave for a further 3–4 minutes. Drain well and return the potatoes to the pan over a low heat for a minute to dry them and to roughen the edges. Carefully transfer them to a roasting tin containing hot oil or dripping. Baste well, then bake at 220°C/425°F/Gas Mark 7 for 20 minutes. Turn them and cook for a further 20–30 minutes, turning and basting at least one more time. Serve as soon as the potatoes are ready.

Potato Croquettes

Mash dry, boiled potatoes with just a little butter or olive oil, then stir in 1 egg yolk mixed with 1–2 tablespoons of milk or crème fraîche to make a firm mixture. Shape the mashed potatoes into small cylinders about 5 cm/2 inches long, rolling them in flour. Dip in beaten egg and then in fresh, white breadcrumbs. Chill the croquettes in the refrigerator for 30 minutes. Place a little unsalted butter and oil in a heavy-based frying pan and slowly heat until the butter has melted. Shallow fry the croquettes, turning occasionally until they are golden brown and crisp.

Rosti

Parboil peeled, waxy potatoes in boiling, salted water for 8 minutes, then drain and leave to cool before coarsely grating into a bowl. Season well with salt and freshly ground black pepper and freshly chopped herbs if liked. Heat a mixture of unsalted butter and oil in a heavy-based frying pan until bubbling. Add tablespoonfuls of

the grated potato into the pan and flatten with the back of a fish slice. Cook over a medium heat for about 7 minutes or until crisp and golden. Turn and cook the other side, then serve while still hot.

Cooking Potatoes in a Clay Pot

Terracotta potato pots can cook up to 450 g/1 lb of whole potatoes at a time. Soak the clay pot for at least 20 minutes before use, then add even-sized, preferably smallish potatoes. Drizzle over a little olive oil and season generously with salt and freshly ground black pepper. Cover the pot with the lid and put in a cold oven, setting the temperature to 200°C/400°F/Gas Mark 6. The potatoes will take about 45 minutes to cook.

Microwaved Potatoes

This method of cooking is suitable for boiling and baking potatoes, providing you do not want the skins to be crispy. To cook new potatoes, prick the skins with a skewer to prevent them from bursting, then place in a bowl with 3 tablespoons of boiling water. Cover with clingfilm which has been pierced two or three times and cook on high for 12–15 minutes, or until tender. Peeled chunks of potato can be cooked in the same way. To bake potatoes, place each potato on a circle of kitchen paper. Make several cuts in each to ensure that the skins do not burst. Transfer to the microwave plate and cook on high for 4–6 minutes per potato, allowing an extra 3–4 minutes for every additional potato. Turn the potatoes at least once during cooking. Leave to stand for 5 minutes before serving.

Health and Nutrition

Potatoes are high in complex carbohydrates, providing sustained energy. They are also an excellent source of vitamins B and C and minerals such as iron and potassium. They contain almost no fat and are high in dietary fibre.

Guidelines for Different Age Groups

Good food plays such an important role in everyone's life. From infancy through to adulthood, a healthy diet provides the body's foundation and building blocks and teaches children healthy eating habits. Studies have shown that these eating habits stay with us into later life helping us to maintain a healthier lifestyle as adults. This reduces the risk of illness, disease and certain medical problems.

Striking a healthy balance is important and at certain stages in life, this balance may need to be adjusted to help our bodies cope. As

babies and children, during pregnancy and in later life, our diet assists us in achieving optimal health. So how do we go about achieving this?

We know that certain foods, such as oily fish, for example, are advantageous to all – they are rich in Omega-3 fatty acids which have been linked with more efficient brain functioning and better memory. They can also help lower the risk of cancer and heart disease. But are there any other steps we can take to maximise health benefits through our diet?

Babies & Young Children

Babies should not be given solids until they are at least six months old, from which point new tastes and textures can be introduced to their diets. Probably the easiest and cheapest way is to adapt the food that the rest of the family eat. Babies under the age of one should be given breast milk or formula. From the age of one to two, whole milk should be given and from two to five semi-skimmed milk can be given. From then on, skimmed milk can be introduced if desired.

The first foods for babies under six months should be of a purée-like consistency, which is smooth and fairly liquid, therefore making it easy to swallow. This can be done using an electric blender or hand blender or just by pushing food through a sieve to remove any lumps. Remember, however, that babies still need high levels of milk.

Babies over six months old should still be having puréed food, but the consistency of their diet can be made progressively lumpier. Around the 10 month mark, most babies are able to manage food cut up into small pieces.

So, what food groups do babies and small children need? Like adults, a high proportion of their diet should contain grains such as cereal, pasta, bread and rice. Be careful, however, as babies and small children cannot cope with too

much high-fibre food in their diet.

Fresh fruits and vegetables should be introduced, as well as a balance of dairy and meat proteins and only a small proportion of fats and sweets. Research points out that delaying the introduction of foods which could cause allergies during the first year (such as cow's milk, wheat, eggs, cheese, yogurt and nuts) can significantly reduce the risk of certain food allergies later on in life. (NB: Peanuts should never be given to children under five years old.)

Seek a doctor or health visitor's advice regarding babies and toddlers. Limit sugar in young children's diets as it provides only empty calories. Use less processed sugars (muscovado is very sweet, so the amount used can be reduced) or incorporate less refined alternatives such as dried fruits, dates, rice syrup or honey. (NB: Honey should not be given to infants under one year of age.)

As in a low-fat diet, it is best to eliminate fried foods and avoid adding salt – especially for under one-year-olds and young infants. Instead, introduce herbs and gentle spices to make food appetising. The more varied the tastes that children experience in their formative years, the wider the range of foods they will accept later in life.

Pregnancy

During pregnancy, women are advised to take extra vitamin and mineral supplements. Pregnant women benefit from a healthy balanced diet, rich in fresh fruit and vegetables, and full of essential vitamins and minerals. Oily fish, such as salmon, not only give the body essential fats but also provide high levels of bio-available calcium.

Certain food groups, however, hold risks during pregnancy. This section gives advice on everyday foods and those that should be avoided.

Cheese

Pregnant women should avoid all soft mould-ripened cheese such as brie. Also, if pregnant, do not eat cheese such as parmesan or blue-veined cheese like stilton as they carry the risk of potential listeria. It is fine for pregnant women to carry on eating hard cheese like cheddar, as well as cottage cheese.

Eggs

There is a slight chance that some eggs will carry salmonella. Cooking the eggs until both the yolk and white are firm will eliminate this risk. However, particular attention should be paid to dishes and products that incorporate lightly cooked or raw eggs, homemade mayonnaise or similar sauces, mousses, soufflés, meringues, ice cream and sorbets. Commercially produced products, such as mayonnaise, are made with pasteurised eggs and may be eaten safely. If in doubt, play safe and avoid it.

Ready-made meals and ready-to-eat items

Previously cooked, then chilled meals are now widely available, but those from the chilled counter can contain bacteria. Avoid prepacked salads in dressings and other foods which are sold loose from chilled cabinets. Also do not eat raw or partly cooked meats, pâté, unpasteurised milk and soil-dirty fruits and vegetables as they can cause toxoplasmosis.

Meat and fish

Certain meats and poultry carry the potential risk of salmonella and should be cooked thoroughly until the juices run clear and there is no pinkness left.

Pay particular attention when buying and cooking fish (especially shellfish). Buy only the freshest fish which should smell salty but not strong or fishy.

Look for bright eyes and reject any with sunken eyes. The bodies should look fresh, plump and shiny. Avoid any fish with dry, shrivelled or damp bodies.

It is also best to avoid any shellfish while pregnant unless it is definitely fresh and thoroughly cooked. Shellfish also contains harmful bacteria and viruses.

Later Life

So what about later on in life? As the body gets older, we can help stave off infection and illness through our diet. There is evidence to show that the immune system becomes weaker as we get older, which can increase the risk of suffering from cancer and other illnesses. Maintaining a diet rich in antioxidants, fresh fruits and vegetables, plant oils and oily fish is especially beneficial in order to either prevent these illnesses or minimise their effects. As with all age groups, the body benefits from the five-a-day eating plan – try to eat five portions of fruit or vegetables each day. Leafy green vegetables, in particular, are rich in antioxidants. Cabbage, broccoli, Brussels sprouts, cauliflower and kale contain particularly high levels of antioxidants, which lower the risk of cancer.

Foods which are green in colour tend to provide nutrients essential for healthy nerves, muscles and hormones, while foods red in colour protect against cardiovascular disease. Other foods that can also assist in preventing cardiovascular disease and ensuring a healthy heart include vitamins E and C, oily fish and essential fats (such as extra virgin olive oil and garlic). They help lower blood cholesterol levels and clear arteries. A diet high in fresh fruits and vegetables and low in salt and saturated fats can considerably reduce heart disease.

Other foods have recognised properties. Certain types of mushrooms are known to boost the immune system, while garlic not only boosts the immune system but also protects the body against cancer. Live yogurt, too, has healthy properties as it contains gut-friendly bacteria which help digestion.

Some foods can help to balance the body's hormone levels during the menopause. For example, soya regulates hormone levels. Studies have shown that a regular intake of soya can help to protect the body against breast and prostate cancer.

A balanced, healthy diet, rich in fresh fruits and vegetables, carbohydrates, proteins and essential fats and low in saturates, can help the body protect itself throughout its life. It really is worth spending a little extra time and effort when shopping or even just thinking about what to cook.

Coriander Chicken & Soy Sauce Cakes

INGREDIENTS

Serves 4

¼ cucumber, peeled

1 shallot, peeled and thinly sliced

6 radishes, trimmed and sliced

350 g/12 oz skinless boneless
   chicken thigh

4 tbsp roughly chopped
   fresh coriander

2 spring onions, trimmed and
   roughly chopped

1 red chilli, deseeded and chopped

finely grated rind of ½ lime

2 tbsp soy sauce

1 tbsp caster sugar

2 tbsp rice vinegar

1 red chilli, deseeded and finely sliced

freshly chopped coriander, to garnish

FOOD FACT

In this recipe, the chicken cakes
can be altered so that half chicken
and half lean pork is used. This
alters the flavour of the dish and
works really well if a small 2.5
cm/1 inch piece of fresh ginger is
grated and added in step 4.

1 Preheat the oven to 190°C/375°F/Gas Mark 5. Halve the cucumber lengthwise, deseed and dice.

2 In a bowl mix the shallot and radishes. Chill until ready to serve with the diced cucumber.

3 Place the chicken thighs in a food processor and blend until coarsely chopped.

4 Add the coriander and spring onions to the chicken with the chilli, lime rind and soy sauce. Blend again until mixed.

5 Using slightly damp hands, shape the chicken mixture into 12 small rounds.

6 Place the rounds on a lightly oiled baking tray and bake in the preheated for 15 minutes, until golden.

7 In a small pan heat the sugar with 2 tablespoons of water until dissolved. Simmer until syrupy.

8 Remove from the heat and allow to cool a little, then stir in the vinegar and chilli slices. Pour over the cucumber and the radish and shallot salad. Garnish with the chopped coriander and serve the chicken cakes with the salad immediately.

2

4

6

Cantonese Chicken Wings

INGREDIENTS

Serves 4

3 tbsp hoisin sauce

2 tbsp dark soy sauce

1 tbsp sesame oil

1 garlic clove, peeled and crushed

2.5 cm/1 inch piece fresh root ginger, peeled and grated

1 tbsp Chinese rice wine or dry sherry

2 tsp chilli bean sauce

2 tsp red or white wine vinegar

2 tbsp soft light brown sugar

900 g/2 lb large chicken wings

50 g/2 oz cashew nuts, chopped

2 spring onions, trimmed and finely chopped

HELPFUL HINT

Chicken wings are regarded as a delicacy in both China and Thailand and are considered one of the tastiest parts of the bird. If you give your butcher advance notice, he will probably sell them to you very cheaply, as they are often trimmed off and discarded when cutting chickens into portions.

1 Preheat the oven to 220°C/425°F/Gas Mark 7, 15 minutes before cooking. Place the hoisin sauce, soy sauce, sesame oil, garlic, ginger, Chinese rice wine or sherry, chilli bean sauce, vinegar and sugar in a small saucepan with 6 tablespoons of water. Bring to the boil, stirring occasionally, then simmer for about 30 seconds. Remove the glaze from the heat.

2 Place the chicken wings in a roasting tin in a single layer. Pour over the glaze and stir until the wings are coated thoroughly.

3 Cover the tin loosely with tinfoil, place in the preheated oven and roast for 25 minutes. Remove the tinfoil, baste the wings and cook for a further 5 minutes.

4 Reduce the oven temperature to 190°C/375°F/Gas Mark 5. Turn the wings over and sprinkle with the chopped cashew nuts and spring onions. Return to the oven and cook for 5 minutes, or until the nuts are lightly browned, the glaze is sticky and the wings are tender. Remove from the oven and leave to stand for 5 minutes before arranging on a warmed platter. Serve immediately with finger bowls and plenty of napkins.

1

2

4

Chicken & Lamb Satay

INGREDIENTS

Makes 16

225 g/8 oz skinless, boneless chicken
225 g/8 oz lean lamb

For the marinade:
1 small onion, peeled and
   finely chopped
2 garlic cloves, peeled and crushed
2.5 cm/1 inch piece fresh root ginger,
   peeled and grated
4 tbsp soy sauce
1 tsp ground coriander
2 tsp dark brown sugar
2 tbsp lime juice
1 tbsp vegetable oil

For the peanut sauce:
300 ml/ ½ pint coconut milk
4 tbsp crunchy peanut butter
1 tbsp Thai fish sauce
1 tsp lime juice
1 tbsp chilli powder
1 tbsp brown sugar
salt and freshly ground black pepper

To garnish:
sprigs of fresh coriander
lime wedges

1. Preheat the grill just before cooking. Soak the bamboo skewers for 30 minutes before required. Cut the chicken and lamb into thin strips, about 7.5 cm/3 inches long and place in 2 shallow dishes. Blend all the marinade ingredients together, then pour half over the chicken and half over the lamb. Stir until lightly coated, then cover with clingfilm and leave to marinate in the refrigerator for at least 2 hours, turning occasionally.

2. Remove the chicken and lamb from the marinade and thread on to the skewers. Reserve the marinade. Cook under the preheated grill for 8–10 minutes or until cooked, turning and brushing with the marinade.

3. Meanwhile, make the peanut sauce. Blend the coconut milk with the peanut butter, fish sauce, lime juice, chilli powder and sugar. Pour into a saucepan and cook gently for 5 minutes, stirring occasionally, then season to taste with salt and pepper. Garnish with coriander sprigs and lime wedges and serve the satays with the prepared sauce.

1

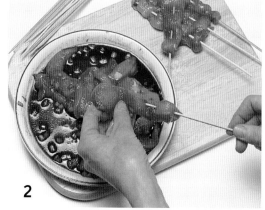

2

3

Chicken Noodle Soup

INGREDIENTS

Serves 4

carcass of a medium-sized
  cooked chicken
1 large carrot, peeled and
  roughly chopped
1 medium onion, peeled
  and quartered
1 leek, trimmed and roughly chopped
2–3 bay leaves
a few black peppercorns
2 litres/3½ pints water
225 g/8 oz Chinese cabbage, trimmed
50 g/2 oz chestnut mushrooms,
  wiped and sliced
125 g/4 oz cooked chicken, sliced
  or chopped
50 g/2 oz medium or fine egg
  thread noodles

1 Break the chicken carcass into smaller pieces and place in the wok with the carrot, onion, leek, bay leaves, peppercorns and water. Bring slowly to the boil. Skim away any fat or scum that rises for the first 15 minutes. Simmer very gently for 1–1½ hours. If the liquid reduces by more than one third, add a little more water.

2 Remove from the heat and leave until cold. Strain into a large bowl and chill in the refrigerator until any fat in the stock rises and sets on the surface. Remove the fat and discard. Draw a sheet of absorbent kitchen paper across the surface of the stock to absorb any remaining fat.

3 Return the stock to the wok and bring to a simmer. Add the Chinese cabbage, mushrooms and chicken and simmer gently for 7–8 minutes until the vegetables are tender.

4 Meanwhile, cook the noodles according to the packet directions until tender. Drain well. Transfer a portion of noodles to each serving bowl before pouring in some soup and vegetables. Serve immediately.

HELPFUL HINT

This is an excellent way to use up any leftover chicken as well as the carcass from a roast chicken.

Chicken–Filled Spring Rolls

INGREDIENTS

Makes 12–14 rolls

For the filling:

1 tbsp vegetable oil

2 slices streaky bacon, diced

225 g/8 oz skinless chicken breast
    fillets, thinly sliced

1 small red pepper, deseeded and
    finely chopped

4 spring onions, trimmed and
    finely chopped

2.5 cm/1 inch piece fresh root ginger,
    peeled and finely chopped

75 g/3 oz mangetout peas,
    thinly sliced

75 g/3 oz beansprouts

1 tbsp soy sauce

2 tsp Chinese rice wine or dry sherry

2 tsp hoisin or plum sauce

For the wrappers:

3 tbsp plain flour

12–14 spring roll wrappers

300 ml/ ½ pint vegetable oil for
    deep frying

shredded spring onions, to garnish

dipping sauce, to serve

1　Heat a large wok, add the oil and when hot add the diced bacon and stir-fry for 2–3 minutes, or until golden. Add the chicken and pepper and stir-fry for a further 2–3 minutes. Add the remaining filling ingredients and stir-fry 3–4 minutes until all the vegetables are tender. Turn into a colander and leave to drain as the mixture cools completely.

2　Blend the flour with about 1½ tablespoons of water to form a paste. Soften each wrapper in a plate of warm water for 1–2 seconds, then place on a chopping board. Put 2–3 tablespoons of filling on the near edge. Fold the edge over the filling to cover. Fold in each side and roll up. Seal the edge with a little flour paste and press to seal securely. Transfer to a baking sheet, seam-side down.

3　Heat the oil in a large wok to 190°C/375°F, or until a small cube of bread browns in about 30 seconds. Working in batches of 3–4, fry the spring rolls until they are crisp and golden, turning once (about 2 minutes). Remove and drain on absorbent kitchen paper. Arrange the spring rolls on a serving plate, garnish with spring onion tassels and serve hot with dipping sauce.

1

2

3

Chicken Wraps

INGREDIENTS

Serves 4

For the stir-fried chicken:

4 skinless chicken breast fillets

finely grated zest and juice of 1 lime

1 tbsp caster sugar

2 tsp dried oregano

1/2 tsp ground cinnamon

1/4 tsp cayenne pepper

3 tbsp sunflower oil

2 onions, peeled and sliced

1 green, 1 red and 1 yellow pepper,
   deseeded and sliced

salt and freshly ground black pepper

For the tortillas:

250 g/9 oz plain flour

pinch of salt

1/4 tsp baking powder

50 g/2 oz white vegetable fat

To serve:

soured cream

guacamole

1 Slice the chicken across the grain into 2 cm/³/₄ inch wide strips. Place in a bowl with the lime zest and juice, sugar, oregano, cinnamon and cayenne pepper. Mix well and leave to marinate while making the tortillas.

2 Sift the flour, salt and baking powder into a bowl. Rub in the white fat, then sprinkle over 4 tablespoons of warm water and mix to a stiff dough. Knead on a lightly floured surface for 10 minutes until smooth and elastic.

3 Divide the dough into 12 equal pieces and roll out each to a 15 cm/6 inch circle. Cover with clingfilm to prevent them drying out before you cook them.

4 Heat a non-stick wok and cook each tortilla for about 1 minute on each side, or until golden and slightly blistered. Remove the tortillas and keep them warm and pliable in a clean tea towel.

5 Heat 2 tablespoons of the oil in the wok and stir-fry the onions for 5 minutes until lightly coloured. Remove with a slotted spoon and reserve.

6 Add the remaining oil to the wok and heat. Drain the chicken from the marinade and add it to the wok. Stir-fry for 5 minutes, then return the onions, add the pepper slices and cook for a further 3–4 minutes, or until the chicken is cooked through and the vegetables are tender. Season to taste with salt and pepper and serve immediately with the tortillas, soured cream and guacamole.

1

4

6

Chinese Chicken Soup

INGREDIENTS

Serves 4

225 g/8 oz cooked chicken

1 tsp oil

6 spring onions, trimmed and
   diagonally sliced

1 red chilli, deseeded and
   finely chopped

1 garlic clove, peeled and crushed

2.5 cm/1 inch piece root ginger,
   peeled and finely grated

1 litre/1³/₄ pint chicken stock

150 g/5 oz medium egg noodles

1 carrot, peeled and cut
   into matchsticks

125 g/4 oz beansprouts

2 tbsp soy sauce

1 tbsp fish sauce

fresh coriander leaves, to garnish

TASTY TIP

Since this soup is stock-based, the use
of corn-fed chicken will make it much
more   flavoursome.   For   added
nutritional   value,   use   wholewheat
noodles and sesame oil. Increase the
vegetable content by adding 75 g/3 oz
each of water chestnuts and bamboo
shoots and 50 g/2 oz of sugar snap
peas and baby corn.

1 Remove any skin from the chicken. Place on a chopping board and
   use two forks to tear the chicken into fine shreds.

2 Heat the oil in a large saucepan and fry the spring onions and chilli
   for 1 minute.

3 Add the garlic and ginger and cook for another minute.

4 Stir in the chicken stock and gradually bring the mixture to the boil.

5 Break up the noodles a little and add to the boiling stock with
   the carrot.

6 Stir to mix, then reduce the heat to a simmer and cook for
   3–4 minutes.

7 Add the shredded chicken, beansprouts, soy sauce and fish sauce
   and stir.

8 Cook for a further 2–3 minutes until piping hot. Ladle the soup into
   bowls and sprinkle with the coriander leaves. Serve immediately.

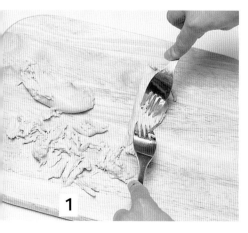

1

5

7

Clear Chicken & Mushroom Soup

INGREDIENTS

Serves 4

2 large chicken legs, about 450 g/1 lb
   total weight
1 tbsp groundnut oil
1 tsp sesame oil
1 onion, peeled and very thinly sliced
2.5 cm/1 inch piece root ginger,
   peeled and very finely chopped
1.1 litres/2 pints clear chicken stock
1 lemon grass stalk, bruised
50 g/2 oz long-grain rice
75 g/3 oz button mushrooms, wiped
   and finely sliced
4 spring onions, trimmed, cut into
   5 cm/2 inch pieces and shredded
1 tbsp dark soy sauce
4 tbsp dry sherry
salt and freshly ground black pepper

1   Skin the chicken legs and remove any fat. Cut each in half to make two thigh and two drumstick portions and reserve. Heat the groundnut and sesame oils in a large saucepan. Add the sliced onion and cook gently for 10 minutes, or until soft but not beginning to colour.

2   Add the chopped ginger to the saucepan and cook for about 30 seconds, stirring all the time to prevent it sticking, then pour in the stock. Add the chicken pieces and the lemon grass, cover and simmer gently for 15 minutes. Stir in the rice and cook for a further 15 minutes or until the chicken is cooked.

3   Remove the chicken from the saucepan and leave until cool enough to handle. Finely shred the flesh, then return to the saucepan with the mushrooms, spring onions, soy sauce and sherry. Simmer for 5 minutes, or until the rice and mushrooms are tender. Remove the lemon grass.

4   Season the soup to taste with salt and pepper. Ladle into warmed serving bowls, making sure each has an equal amount of shredded chicken and vegetables and serve immediately.

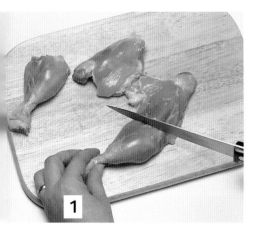

1

2

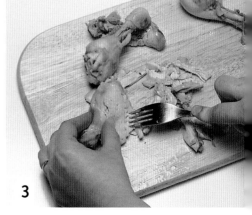

3

Creamy Chicken & Tofu Soup

INGREDIENTS

Serves 4–6

225 g/8 oz firm tofu, drained

3 tbsp groundnut oil

1 garlic clove, peeled and crushed

2.5 cm/1 inch piece root ginger,
   peeled and finely chopped

2.5 cm/1 inch piece fresh galangal,
   peeled and finely sliced (if available)

1 lemon grass stalk, bruised

¼ tsp ground turmeric

600 ml/1 pint chicken stock

600 ml/1 pint coconut milk

225 g/8 oz cauliflower, cut into
   tiny florets

1 medium carrot, peeled and cut into
   thin matchsticks

125 g/4 oz green beans, trimmed and
   cut in half

75 g/3 oz thin egg noodles

225 g/8 oz cooked chicken, shredded

salt and freshly ground black pepper

1 Cut the tofu into 1 cm/½ inch cubes, then pat dry on absorbent kitchen paper.

2 Heat 1 tablespoon of the oil in a nonstick frying pan. Fry the tofu in 2 batches for 3–4 minutes or until golden brown. Remove, drain on absorbent kitchen paper and reserve.

3 Heat the remaining oil in a large saucepan. Add the garlic, ginger, galangal and lemon grass and cook for about 30 seconds. Stir in the turmeric, then pour in the stock and coconut milk and bring to the boil. Reduce the heat to a gentle simmer, add the cauliflower and carrots and simmer for 10 minutes. Add the green beans and simmer for a further 5 minutes.

4 Meanwhile, bring a large saucepan of lightly salted water to the boil. Add the noodles, turn off the heat, cover and leave to cook or cook according to the packet instructions.

5 Remove the lemon grass from the soup. Drain the noodles and stir into the soup with the chicken and browned tofu. Season to taste with salt and pepper, then simmer gently for 2–3 minutes or until heated through. Serve immediately in warmed soup bowls.

FOOD FACT

Tofu is a white curd made from soya beans. It originated in China and is made in a similar way to cheese.

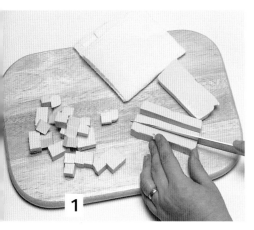

1

2

3

Crostini with Chicken Livers

INGREDIENTS

Serves 4

2 tbsp olive oil

2 tbsp butter

1 shallot, peeled and finely chopped

1 garlic clove, peeled and crushed

150 g/5 oz chicken livers

1 tbsp plain flour

2 tbsp dry white wine

1 tbsp brandy

50 g/2 oz mushrooms, sliced

salt and freshly ground black pepper

4 slices of ciabatta or similar bread

To garnish:

fresh sage leaves

lemon wedges

TASTY TIP

If you prefer a lower fat alternative to the fried bread in this recipe, omit 1 tablespoon of the butter and brush the bread slices with the remaining 1 tablespoon of oil. Bake in a preheated oven 180°C/350°F/Gas Mark 4 for about 20 minutes, or until golden and crisp then serve as above.

1 Heat 1 tablespoon of the olive oil and 1 tablespoon of the butter in a frying pan, add the shallot and garlic and cook gently for 2–3 minutes.

2 Trim and wash the chicken livers thoroughly and pat dry on absorbent kitchen paper as much as possible. Cut into slices, then toss in the flour. Add the livers to the frying pan with the shallot and garlic and continue to fry for a further 2 minutes, stirring continuously.

3 Pour in the white wine and brandy and bring to the boil. Boil rapidly for 1–2 minutes to allow the alcohol to evaporate, then stir in the sliced mushrooms and cook gently for about 5 minutes, or until the chicken livers are cooked, but just a little pink inside. Season to taste with salt and pepper.

4 Fry the slices of ciabatta or similar-style bread in the remaining oil and butter, then place on individual serving dishes. Spoon over the liver mixture and garnish with a few sage leaves and lemon wedges. Serve immediately.

2

3

3

Garlic Mushrooms with Crispy Bacon & Chicken Liver Sauté

INGREDIENTS

Serves 4

4 large field mushrooms

40 g/1½ oz butter, melted and cooled

2 garlic cloves, peeled and crushed

1 tbsp sunflower oil

3 rashers smoked streaky bacon,
  derinded and chopped

4 shallots, peeled and thinly sliced

450 g/1 lb chicken livers, halved

2 tbsp marsala or sweet sherry

4 tbsp chicken or vegetable stock

6 tbsp double cream

2 tsp freshly chopped thyme

salt and freshly ground black pepper

1 Remove the stalks from the mushrooms and roughly chop. Mix together 25 g/1 oz of the butter and garlic and brush over both sides of the mushroom caps. Place on the rack of a grill pan.

2 Heat a wok, add the oil and when hot, add the bacon and stir-fry for 2–3 minutes, or until crispy. Remove and reserve. Add the remaining butter to the wok and stir-fry the shallots and chopped mushroom stalks for 4–5 minutes until they are softened.

3 Add the chicken livers and cook for 3–4 minutes, or until well browned on the outside, but still pink and tender inside. Pour in the marsala or sherry and the stock. Simmer for 1 minute, then stir in the cream, thyme, salt and pepper and half the bacon. Cook for about 30 seconds to heat through.

4 While the livers are frying, cook the mushroom caps under a hot grill for 3–4 minutes each side, until tender.

5 Place the mushrooms on warmed serving plates, allowing 1 per person. Spoon the chicken livers over and around the mushrooms. Scatter with the remaining bacon and serve immediately.

1

2

3

Hoisin Chicken Pancakes

INGREDIENTS

Serves 4

3 tbsp hoisin sauce
1 garlic clove, peeled and crushed
2.5 cm/1 inch piece root ginger,
   peeled and finely grated
1 tbsp soy sauce
1 tsp sesame oil
salt and freshly ground black pepper
4 skinless chicken thighs
½ cucumber, peeled (optional)
12 bought Chinese pancakes
6 spring onions, trimmed and cut
   lengthways into fine shreds
sweet chilli dipping sauce, to serve

TASTY TIP

For those with wheat allergies or who want to make this tasty dish more substantial, stir-fry the spring onions and cucumber batons in a little groundnut oil. Add a carrot cut into batons and mix in the thinly sliced chicken and reserved marinade. Serve with steamed rice – Thai fragrant rice is particularly good.

1 Preheat the oven to 190°C/375°F/Gas Mark 5. In a non-metallic bowl, mix the hoisin sauce with the garlic, ginger, soy sauce, sesame oil and seasoning.

2 Add the chicken thighs and turn to coat in the mixture. Cover loosely and leave in the refrigerator to marinate for 3–4 hours, turning the chicken from time to time.

3 Remove the chicken from the marinade and place in a roasting tin. Reserve the marinade. Bake in the preheated oven for 30 minutes basting occasionally with the marinade.

4 Cut the cucumber in half lengthways and remove the seeds by running a teaspoon down the middle to scoop them out. Cut into thin batons.

5 Place the pancakes in a steamer to warm or heat according to packet instructions. Thinly slice the hot chicken and arrange on a plate with the shredded spring onions, cucumber and pancakes.

6 Place a spoonful of the chicken in the middle of each warmed pancake and top with pieces of cucumber, spring onion, and a little dipping sauce. Roll up and serve immediately.

2

4

5

Laksa Malayan Rice Noodle Soup

INGREDIENTS

Serves 4–6

1.1 kg/2½ lb corn-fed,
  free-range chicken
1 tsp black peppercorns
1 tbsp vegetable oil
1 large onion, peeled and thinly sliced
2 garlic cloves, peeled and
  finely chopped
2.5 cm/1 inch piece fresh root ginger,
  peeled and thinly sliced
1 tsp ground coriander
2 red chillies, deseeded and
  diagonally sliced
1–2 tsp hot curry paste
400 ml/14 fl oz coconut milk
450 g/1 lb large raw prawns, peeled
  and deveined
½ small head of Chinese leaves,
  thinly shredded
1 tsp sugar
2 spring onions, trimmed and
  thinly sliced
125 g/4 oz beansprouts
250 g/9 oz rice noodles or rice sticks,
  soaked as per packet instructions
fresh mint leaves, to garnish

1 Put the chicken in a large saucepan with the peppercorns and cover with cold water. Bring to the boil, skimming off any scum that rises to the surface. Simmer, partially covered, for about 1 hour. Remove the chicken and cool. Skim any fat from the stock and strain through a muslin-lined sieve and reserve. Remove the meat from the carcass, shred and reserve.

2 Heat a large wok, add the oil and when hot, add the onions and stir-fry for 2 minutes, or until they begin to colour. Stir in the garlic, ginger, coriander, chillies and curry paste and stir-fry for a further 2 minutes.

3 Carefully pour in the reserved stock (you need at least 1.1 litres/2 pints) and simmer gently, partially covered, for 10 minutes, or until slightly reduced.

4 Add the coconut milk, prawns, Chinese leaves, sugar, spring onions and beansprouts and simmer for 3 minutes, stirring occasionally. Add the reserved shredded chicken, and cook for a further 2 minutes.

5 Drain the noodles and divide between 4–6 soup bowls. Ladle the hot stock and vegetables over the noodles, making sure each serving has some prawns and chicken. Garnish each bowl with fresh mint leaves and serve immediately.

1

2

4

Oriental Minced Chicken on Rocket & Tomato

INGREDIENTS

Serves 4

2 shallots, peeled

1 garlic clove, peeled

1 carrot, peeled

50 g/2 oz water chestnuts

1 tsp oil

350 g/12 oz fresh chicken mince

1 tsp Chinese five spice powder

pinch chilli powder

1 tsp soy sauce

1 tbsp fish sauce

8 cherry tomatoes

50 g/2 oz rocket

TASTY TIP

This is a very versatile dish. In place of the chicken you could use any lean cut of meat or even prawns. To make this dish a main meal replace the rocket and tomatoes with stir-fried vegetables and rice. Another alternative that works very well is to serve the chicken mixture in step 3 in lettuce leaves. Place a spoonful of the mixture into a lettuce leaf and roll up into a small parcel.

1 Finely chop the shallots and garlic. Cut the carrot into matchsticks, thinly slice the water chestnuts and reserve. Heat the oil in a wok or heavy-based large frying pan and add the chicken. Stir-fry for 3–4 minutes over a moderately high heat, breaking up any large pieces of chicken.

2 Add the garlic and shallots and cook for 2–3 minutes until softened. Sprinkle over the Chinese five spice powder and the chilli powder and continue to cook for about 1 minute.

3 Add the carrot, water chestnuts, soy and fish sauce and 2 tablespoons of water. Stir-fry for a further 2 minutes. Remove from the heat and reserve to cool slightly.

4 De-seed the tomatoes and cut into thin wedges. Toss with the rocket and divide between four serving plates. Spoon the warm chicken mixture over the rocket and tomato wedges and serve immediately to prevent the rocket from wilting.

1

1

4

Spicy Chicken Skewers with Mango Tabbouleh

INGREDIENTS

Serves 4

400 g/14 oz chicken breast fillet
200 ml/7 fl oz natural low fat yogurt
1 garlic clove, peeled and crushed
1 small red chilli, deseeded and
 finely chopped
½ tsp ground turmeric
finely grated rind and juice of
 ½ lemon
sprigs of fresh mint, to garnish

Mango tabbouleh:

175 g/6 oz bulgur wheat
1 tsp olive oil
juice of ½ lemon
½ red onion, finely chopped
1 ripe mango, halved, stoned, peeled
 and chopped
¼ cucumber, finely diced
2 tbsp freshly chopped parsley
2 tbsp freshly shredded mint
salt and finely ground black pepper

1 If using wooden skewers, pre-soak them in cold water for at least 30 minutes. (This stops them from burning during grilling.)

2 Cut the chicken into 5 x 1 cm/2 x ½ inch strips and place in a shallow dish.

3 Mix together the yogurt, garlic, chilli, turmeric, lemon rind and juice. Pour over the chicken and toss to coat. Cover and leave to marinate in the refrigerator for up to 8 hours.

4 To make the tabbouleh, put the bulgur wheat in a bowl. Pour over enough boiling water to cover. Put a plate over the bowl. Leave to soak for 20 minutes.

5 Whisk together the oil and lemon juice in a bowl. Add the red onion and leave to marinade for 10 minutes.

6 Drain the bulgur wheat and squeeze out any excess moisture in a clean tea towel. Add to the red onion with the mango, cucumber, herbs and season to taste with salt and pepper. Toss together.

7 Thread the chicken strips on to 8 wooden or metal skewers. Cook under a hot grill for 8 minutes. Turn and brush with the marinade, until the chicken is lightly browned and cooked through.

8 Spoon the tabbouleh on to individual plates. Arrange the chicken skewers on top and garnish with the sprigs of mint. Serve warm or cold.

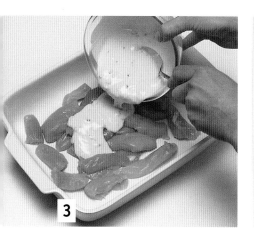

3

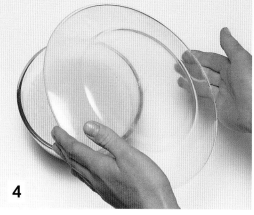

4

6

Thai Stir-Fried Spicy Turkey

INGREDIENTS

Serves 4

2 tbsp Thai fragrant rice
2 tbsp lemon juice
3–5 tbsp chicken stock
2 tbsp Thai fish sauce
½–1 tsp cayenne pepper, or to taste
125 g/4 oz fresh turkey mince
2 shallots, peeled and chopped
½ lemon grass stalk, outer leaves
   discarded and finely sliced
1 lime leaf, finely sliced
1 spring onion, trimmed and
   finely chopped
freshly chopped coriander, to garnish
Chinese leaves, to serve

TASTY TIP

Cooking the rice before grinding, gives it a nutty, toasted flavour. Take care to only cook it until lightly browned and not at all blackened, as this would spoil the flavour. Chinese leaves make great serving containers and enable this dish to be eaten with fingers. It would also make a delicious starter for 6 to 8 people.

1   Place the rice in a small frying pan and cook, stirring constantly, over a medium high heat for 4–5 minutes, or until the rice is browned. Transfer to a spice grinder or blender and pulse briefly until roughly ground. Reserve.

2   Place the lemon juice, 3 tablespoons of the stock, the fish sauce and cayenne pepper into a small saucepan and bring to the boil. Add the turkey mince and return to the boil. Continue cooking over a high heat until the turkey is sealed all over.

3   Add the shallots to the saucepan with the lemon grass, lime leaf, spring onion and reserved rice. Continue cooking for another 1–2 minutes, or until the turkey is cooked through, adding a little more stock, if necessary to keep the mixture moist.

4   Spoon a little of the mixture into each Chinese leaf and arrange on a serving dish or individual plates. Garnish with a little chopped coriander and serve immediately.

Wonton Soup

INGREDIENTS

Serves 6

For the chicken stock:

900 g/2 lb chicken or chicken pieces
  with back, feet and wings
1–2 onions, peeled and quartered
2 carrots, peeled and chopped
2 celery stalks, trimmed and chopped
1 leek, trimmed and chopped
2 garlic cloves, unpeeled and
  lightly crushed
1 tbsp black peppercorns
2 bay leaves
small bunch parsley, stems only
2–3 slices fresh root ginger,
  peeled (optional)
3.4 litres/6 pints cold water

For the soup:

18 wontons
2–3 Chinese leaves, or a handful of
  spinach, shredded
1 small carrot, peeled and cut
  into matchsticks
2–4 spring onions, trimmed and
  diagonally sliced
soy sauce, to taste
handful flat leaf parsley, to garnish

1 Chop the chicken into 6–8 pieces and put into a large stock pot or saucepan of water with the remaining stock ingredients. Place over a high heat and bring to the boil, skimming off any scum which rises to the surface. Reduce the heat and simmer for 2–3 hours, skimming occasionally.

2 Strain the stock through a fine sieve or muslin-lined sieve into a large bowl. Leave to cool, then chill in the refrigerator for 5–6 hours, or overnight. When cold, skim off the fat and remove any small pieces of fat by dragging a piece of absorbent kitchen paper lightly across the surface.

3 Bring a medium saucepan of water to the boil. Add the wontons and return to the boil. Simmer for 2–3 minutes, or until the wontons are cooked, stir frequently. Rinse under cold running water, drain and reserve.

4 Pour 300 ml/½ pint stock per person into a large wok. Bring to the boil over a high heat, skimming any foam that rises to the surface and simmer for 5–7 minutes to reduce slightly. Add the wontons, Chinese leaves or spinach, carrots and spring onions. Season with a few drops of soy sauce and simmer for 2–3 minutes. Garnish with a few parsley leaves and serve immediately.

Chicken Cacciatore

INGREDIENTS

Serves 4

4 chicken leg portions

1 tbsp olive oil

1 red onion, peeled and cut into very
   thin wedges

1 garlic clove, peeled and crushed

sprig of fresh thyme

sprig of fresh rosemary

150 ml/¼ pint dry white wine

200 ml/7 fl oz chicken stock

400 g can chopped tomatoes

40 g/1½ oz black olives, pitted

15 g/½ oz capers, drained

salt and freshly ground black pepper

freshly cooked fettuccine, linguine or
   pasta shells

HELPFUL HINT

When watching your saturated fat intake, it is essential to remove the skin from the chicken before eating. Any fat is deposited directly underneath the skin.

1 Skin the chicken portions and cut each one into two pieces to make four thighs and four drumsticks.

2 Heat 2 teaspoons of the oil in a flameproof casserole and cook the chicken for 2–3 minutes on each side until lightly browned. Remove the chicken from the pan and reserve.

3 Add the remaining 1 teaspoon of oil to the juices in the pan.

4 Add the red onion and gently cook for 5 minutes, stirring occasionally.

5 Add the garlic and cook for a further 5 minutes until soft and beginning to brown. Return the chicken to the pan.

6 Add the herbs, then pour in the wine and let it bubble for 1–2 minutes.

7 Add the stock and tomatoes, cover and gently simmer for 15 minutes.

8 Stir in the olives and capers. Cook uncovered for a further 5 minutes or until the chicken is cooked and the sauce thickened. Remove the herbs and season to taste with salt and pepper.

9 Place the chicken on a bed of pasta, allowing one thigh and one drumstick per person. Spoon over the sauce and serve.

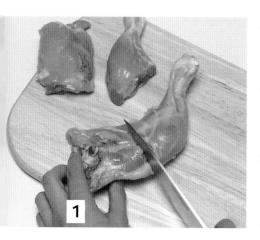

Chicken Basquaise

INGREDIENTS

Serves 4–6

1.4 kg/3 lb chicken, cut into 8 pieces
2 tbsp plain flour
salt and freshly ground black pepper
3 tbsp olive oil
1 large onion, peeled and sliced
2 red peppers, deseeded and cut into
  thick strips
2 garlic cloves, peeled and crushed
150 g/5 oz spicy chorizo sausage cut
  into 1 cm/½ inch pieces
200 g/7 oz long-grain white rice
450 ml/¾ pint chicken stock
1 tsp crushed dried chillies
½ tsp dried thyme
1 tbsp tomato purée
125 g/4 oz Spanish air-dried
  ham, diced
12 black olives
2 tbsp freshly chopped parsley

1 Dry the chicken pieces well with absorbent kitchen paper. Put the flour in a polythene bag, season with salt and pepper and add the chicken pieces. Twist the bag to seal, then shake to coat the chicken pieces thoroughly.

2 Heat 2 tablespoons of the oil in a large heavy-based saucepan over a medium-high heat. Add the chicken pieces and cook for about 15 minutes, turning on all sides, until well browned. Using a slotted spoon, transfer to a plate.

3 Add the remaining olive oil to the saucepan, then add the onion and peppers. Reduce the heat to medium and cook, stirring frequently, until starting to colour and soften. Stir in the garlic and chorizo and continue to cook for a further 3 minutes. Add the rice and cook for about 2 minutes, stirring to coat with the oil, until the rice is translucent and golden.

4 Stir in the stock, crushed chillies, thyme, tomato purée and salt and pepper and bring to the boil. Return the chicken to the saucepan, pressing gently into the rice. Cover and cook over a very low heat for about 45 minutes until the chicken and rice are cooked and tender.

5 Gently stir in the ham, black olives and half the parsley. Cover and heat for a further 5 minutes. Sprinkle with the remaining parsley and serve immediately.

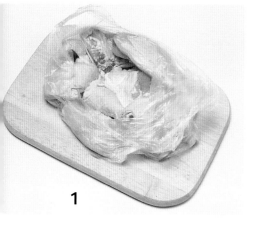

1

3

5

Braised Chicken in Beer

INGREDIENTS

Serves 4

4 chicken joints, skinned
125 g/4 oz pitted dried prunes
2 bay leaves
12 shallots
2 tsp olive oil
125 g/4 oz small button mushrooms,
  wiped
1 tsp soft dark brown sugar
½ tsp whole-grain mustard
2 tsp tomato purée
150 ml/ ¼ pint light ale
150 ml/ ¼ pint chicken stock
salt and freshly ground black pepper
2 tsp cornflour
2 tsp lemon juice
2 tbsp chopped fresh parsley
flat-leaf parsley, to garnish

To serve

mashed potatoes
seasonal green vegetables

1   Preheat the oven to 170°C/325°F/Gas Mark 3. Cut each chicken joint in half and put in an ovenproof casserole with the prunes and bay leaves.

2   To peel the shallots, put in a small bowl and cover with boiling water.

3   Drain the shallots after 2 minutes and rinse under cold water until cool enough to handle. The skins should then peel away easily from the shallots.

4   Heat the oil in a large non-stick frying pan. Add the shallots and gently cook for about 5 minutes until beginning to colour.

5   Add the mushrooms to the pan and cook for a further 3–4 minutes until both the mushrooms and onions are softened.

6   Sprinkle the sugar over the shallots and mushrooms, then add the mustard, tomato purée, ale and chicken stock. Season to taste with salt and pepper and bring to the boil, stirring to combine. Carefully pour over the chicken.

7   Cover the casserole and cook in the preheated oven for 1 hour. Blend the cornflour with the lemon juice and 1 tablespoon of cold water and stir into the chicken casserole.

8   Return the casserole to the oven for a further 10 minutes or until the chicken is cooked and the vegetables are tender.

9   Remove the bay leaves and stir in the chopped parsley. Garnish the chicken with the flat-leaf parsley. Serve with the mashed potatoes and fresh green vegetables.

1

5

6

Chicken Baked in a Salt Crust

INGREDIENTS

Serves 4

1.8 kg/4 lb oven-ready chicken
salt and freshly ground black pepper
1 medium onion, peeled
sprig of fresh rosemary
sprig of fresh thyme
1 bay leaf
15 g/ ½ oz butter, softened
1 garlic clove, peeled and crushed
pinch of ground paprika
finely grated rind of ½ lemon

To garnish:
fresh herbs
lemon slices

For the salt crust:
900 g/2 lb plain flour
450 g/1 lb fine cooking salt
450 g/1 lb coarse sea salt
2 tbsp oil

HELPFUL HINT

It is best to avoid eating the skin from the chicken. It is high in fat and also absorbs a lot of salt from the crust.

1 Preheat the oven to 170°C/325°F/Gas Mark 3. Remove the giblets if necessary and rinse the chicken with cold water. Sprinkle the inside with salt and pepper. Put the onion inside with the rosemary, thyme and bay leaf.

2 Mix the butter, garlic, paprika and lemon rind together. Starting at the neck end, gently ease the skin from the chicken and push the mixture under.

3 To make the salt crust, put the flour and salts in a large mixing bowl and stir together. Make a well in the centre. Pour in 600 ml/1 pint of cold water and the oil. Mix to a stiff dough, then knead on a lightly floured surface for 2–3 minutes. Roll out the pastry to a circle with a diameter of about 51 cm/20 inches. Place the chicken breast side down in the middle. Lightly brush the edges with water, then fold over to enclose. Pinch the joints together to seal.

4 Put the chicken join side down in a roasting tin and cook in the preheated oven for 2 ¾ hours. Remove from the oven and stand for 20 minutes.

5 Break open the hard crust and remove the chicken. Discard the crust. Remove the skin from the chicken, garnish with the fresh herbs and lemon slices. Serve the chicken immediately.

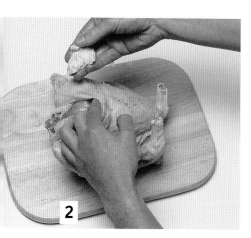

2

3

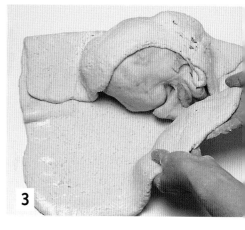

3

Paella

INGREDIENTS

Serves 6

450 g/1 lb live mussels
4 tbsp olive oil
6 medium chicken thighs
1 medium onion, peeled and
  finely chopped
1 garlic clove, peeled and crushed
225 g/8 oz tomatoes, skinned,
  deseeded and chopped
1 red pepper, deseeded and chopped
1 green pepper, deseeded
  and chopped
125 g/4 oz frozen peas
1 tsp paprika
450 g/1 lb Arborio rice
½ tsp turmeric
900 ml/1½ pints chicken
  stock, warmed
175 g/6 oz large peeled prawns
salt and freshly ground black pepper
2 limes
1 lemon
1 tbsp freshly chopped basil
whole cooked unpeeled prawns,
  to garnish

1   Rinse the mussels under cold running water, scrubbing well to remove any grit and barnacles, then pull off the hairy 'beards'. Tap any open mussels sharply with a knife, and discard if they refuse to close.

2   Heat the oil in a paella pan or large, heavy-based frying pan and cook the chicken thighs for 10–15 minutes until golden. Remove and keep warm.

3   Fry the onion and garlic in the remaining oil in the pan for 2–3 minutes, then add the tomatoes, peppers, peas and paprika and cook for a further 3 minutes.

4   Add the rice to the pan and return the chicken with the turmeric and half the stock. Bring to the boil and simmer, gradually adding more stock as it is absorbed. Cook for 20 minutes, or until most of the stock has been absorbed and the rice is almost tender.

5   Put the mussels in a large saucepan with 5 cm/2 inches boiling salted water, cover and steam for 5 minutes. Discard any with shells that have not opened, then stir into the rice with the prawns. Season to taste with salt and pepper. Heat through for 2–3 minutes until piping hot. Squeeze the juice from 1 of the limes over the paella.

6   Cut the remaining limes and the lemon into wedges and arrange on top of the paella. Sprinkle with the basil, garnish with the prawns and serve.

2

4

5

Creamy Chicken Stroganoff

INGREDIENTS

Serves 4

450 g/1 lb skinless chicken breast fillets
4 tbsp dry sherry
15 g/ ½ oz dried porcini mushrooms
2 tbsp sunflower oil
25 g/1 oz unsalted butter
1 onion, peeled and sliced
225 g/8 oz chestnut mushrooms,
   wiped and sliced
1 tbsp paprika
1 tsp freshly chopped thyme
125 ml/4 fl oz chicken stock
150 ml/ ¼ pint crème fraîche
salt and freshly ground black pepper

To serve:
crème fraîche
freshly cooked rice or
   egg noodles
sprigs of fresh thyme, to garnish

HELPFUL HINT

Dried porcini mushrooms should be soaked in very hot, but not boiling water for at least 20 minutes. Use the soaking liquor as well as the rehydrated mushrooms in order to obtain maximum flavour from the mushrooms.

1   Cut the chicken into finger-length strips and reserve. Gently warm the sherry in a small saucepan and remove from the heat. Add the porcini mushrooms and leave to soak while preparing the rest of the stir-fry.

2   Heat a wok, add 1½ tablespoons of the oil and when hot, add the chicken and stir-fry over a high heat for 3–4 minutes, or until lightly browned. Remove from the wok and reserve.

3   Heat the remaining oil and butter in the wok and gently cook the onion for 5 minutes. Add the chestnut mushrooms and stir-fry for a further 5 minutes, or until tender. Sprinkle in the paprika and thyme and cook for 30 seconds.

4   Add the porcini mushrooms with their soaking liquid, then stir in the stock and return the chicken to the wok. Cook for 1–2 minutes, or until the chicken is cooked through and tender.

5   Stir in the crème fraîche and heat until piping hot. Season to taste with salt and pepper. Garnish with sprigs of fresh thyme and serve immediately with a spoonful of crème fraîche and rice or egg noodles.

1

2

3

Potato–Stuffed Roast Poussin

INGREDIENTS

Serves 4

4 oven-ready poussins
salt and freshly ground black pepper
1 lemon, cut into quarters
450 g/1 lb floury potatoes, peeled and
  cut into 4 cm/1½ inch pieces
1 tbsp freshly chopped thyme
  or rosemary
3–4 tbsp olive oil
4 garlic cloves, unpeeled and
  lightly smashed
8 slices streaky bacon or Parma ham
125 ml/4 fl oz white wine
2 spring onions, trimmed and
  thinly sliced
2 tbsp double cream or crème fraîche
lemon wedges, to garnish

1 Preheat the oven to 220°C/425°F/Gas Mark 7. Place a roasting tin in the oven to heat. Rinse the poussin cavities and pat dry with absorbent kitchen paper. Season the cavities with salt and pepper and a squeeze of lemon. Push a lemon quarter into each cavity.

2 Put the potatoes in a saucepan of lightly salted water and bring to the boil. Reduce the heat to low and simmer until just tender; do not overcook. Drain and cool slightly. Sprinkle the chopped herbs over the potatoes and drizzle with 2–3 tablespoons of the oil.

3 Spoon half the seasoned potatoes into the poussin cavities; do not pack too tightly. Rub each poussin with a little more oil and season with pepper. Carefully spoon 1 tablespoon of oil into the hot roasting tin and arrange the poussins in the tin. Spoon the remaining potatoes around the edge. Sprinkle over the garlic.

4 Roast the poussins in the preheated oven for 30 minutes, or until the skin is golden and beginning to crisp. Carefully lay the bacon slices over the breast of each poussin and continue to roast for 15–20 minutes until crisp and the poussins are cooked through.

5 Transfer the poussins and potatoes to a serving platter and cover loosely with tinfoil. Skim off the fat from the juices. Place the tin over a medium heat, add the wine and spring onions. Cook briefly, scraping the bits from the bottom of the tin. Whisk in the cream or crème fraîche and bubble for 1 minute, or until thickened. Garnish the poussins with lemon wedges, and serve with the creamy gravy.

2

3

4

Saffron Roast Chicken with Crispy Onions

INGREDIENTS

Serves 4–6

1.6 kg/3½ lb oven-ready chicken,
  preferably free range
75 g/3 oz butter, softened
1 tsp saffron strands, lightly toasted
grated rind of 1 lemon
2 tbsp freshly chopped flat-leaf parsley
2 tbsp extra-virgin olive oil
450 g/1 lb onions, peeled and cut into
  thin wedges
8–12 garlic cloves, peeled
1 tsp cumin seeds
½ tsp ground cinnamon
50 g/2 oz pine nuts
50 g/2 oz sultanas
salt and freshly ground black pepper
sprig of fresh flat-leaf parsley,
  to garnish

1 Preheat oven to 200°C/400°F/Gas Mark 6. Using your fingertips, gently loosen the skin from the chicken breast by sliding your hand between the skin and flesh. Cream together 50 g/2 oz of the butter with the saffron threads, the lemon rind and half the parsley, until smooth. Push the butter under the skin. Spread over the breast and the top of the thighs with your fingers. Pull the neck skin to tighten the skin over the breast and tuck under the bird, then secure with a skewer or cocktail stick.

2 Heat the olive oil and remaining butter in a large heavy-based frying pan and cook the onions and garlic cloves for 5 minutes, or until the onions are soft. Stir in the cumin seeds, cinnamon, pine nuts and sultanas and cook for 2 minutes. Season to taste with salt and pepper and place in a roasting tin.

3 Place the chicken, breast-side down, on the base of the onions and roast in the preheated oven for 45 minutes. Reduce the oven temperature to 170°C/325°F/Gas Mark 3. Turn the chicken breast-side up and stir the onions. Continue roasting until the chicken is a deep golden yellow and the onions are crisp. Allow to rest for 10 minutes, then sprinkle with the remaining parsley. Before serving, garnish with a sprig of parsley and serve immediately with the onions and garlic.

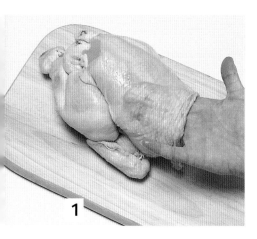

1

1

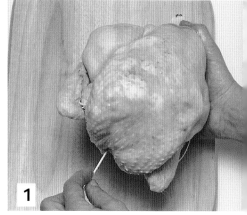

1

Turkey & Pesto Rice Roulades

INGREDIENTS

Serves 4

125 g/4 oz cooked white rice,
  at room temperature
1 garlic clove, peeled and crushed
1–2 tbsp Parmesan cheese, grated
2 tbsp prepared pesto sauce
2 tbsp pine nuts, lightly toasted
  and chopped
4 turkey steaks, each weighing about
  150 g/5 oz
salt and freshly ground black pepper
4 slices Parma ham
2 tbsp olive oil
50 ml/2 fl oz white wine
25 g/1 oz unsalted butter, chilled

To serve:
freshly cooked spinach
freshly cooked pasta

1. Put the rice in a bowl and add the garlic, Parmesan cheese, pesto and pine nuts. Stir to combine the ingredients, then reserve.

2. Place the turkey steaks on a chopping board and, using a sharp knife, cut horizontally through each steak, without cutting right through. Open up the steaks and cover with baking parchment. Flatten slightly by pounding with a meat mallet or rolling pin.

3. Season each steak with salt and pepper. Divide the stuffing equally among the steaks, spreading evenly over one half. Fold the steaks in half to enclose the filling, then wrap each steak in a slice of Parma ham and secure with cocktail sticks.

4. Heat the oil in a large frying pan over medium heat. Cook the steaks for 5 minutes, or until golden on one side. Turn and cook for a further 2 minutes. Push the steaks to the side and pour in the wine. Allow the wine to bubble and evaporate. Add the butter, a little at a time, whisking constantly until the sauce is smooth. Discard the cocktail sticks, then serve the steaks drizzled with the sauce and serve with spinach and pasta.

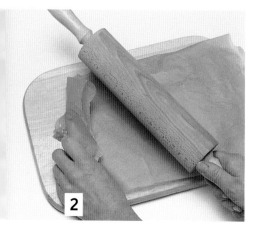

2

3

4

Slow Roast Chicken with Potatoes & Oregano

INGREDIENTS

Serves 6

1.4–1.8 kg/3–4 lb oven-ready chicken, preferably free range

1 lemon, halved

1 onion, peeled and quartered

50 g/2 oz butter, softened

salt and freshly ground black pepper

1 kg/2¼ lb potatoes, peeled and quartered

3–4 tbsp extra virgin olive oil

1 tbsp dried oregano, crumbled

1 tsp fresh thyme leaves

2 tbsp freshly chopped thyme

fresh sage leaves, to garnish

1   Preheat the oven to 200°C/400°F/Gas Mark 6. Rinse the chicken and dry well, inside and out, with absorbent kitchen paper. Rub the chicken all over with the lemon halves, then squeeze the juice over it and into the cavity. Put the squeezed halves into the cavity with the quartered onion.

2   Rub the softened butter all over the chicken and season to taste with salt and pepper, then put it in a large roasting tin, breast-side down.

3   Toss the potatoes in the oil, season with salt and pepper to taste and add the dried oregano and fresh thyme. Arrange the potatoes with the oil around the chicken and carefully pour 150 ml/¼ pint water into one end of the pan (not over the oil).

4   Roast in the preheated oven for 25 minutes. Reduce the oven temperature to 190°C/375°F/Gas Mark 5 and turn the chicken breast-side up. Turn the potatoes, sprinkle over half the fresh herbs and baste the chicken and potatoes with the juices. Continue roasting for 1 hour, or until the chicken is cooked, basting occasionally. If the liquid evaporates completely, add a little more water. The chicken is done when the juices run clear when the thigh is pierced with a skewer.

5   Transfer the chicken to a carving board and rest for 5 minutes, covered with tinfoil. Return the potatoes to the oven while the chicken is resting.

6   Carve the chicken into serving pieces and arrange on a large heatproof serving dish. Arrange the potatoes around the chicken and drizzle over any remaining juices. Sprinkle with the remaining herbs and serve.

3

4

4

Fruity Rice-Stuffed Poussins

INGREDIENTS

Serves 6

6 oven-ready poussins
50 g/2 oz butter, melted

For the rice stuffing:

225 ml/8 fl oz port
125 g/4 oz raisins
125 g/4 oz dried apricots, chopped
2 tbsp olive oil
1 medium onion, peeled and chopped
1 celery stalk, trimmed and sliced
2 garlic cloves, peeled and
  finely chopped
1½ tsp mixed spice
1 tsp each dried oregano and mint
225 g/8 oz unsweetened canned
  chestnuts, chopped
200 g/7 oz long-grain white
  rice, cooked
grated rind and juice of 2 oranges
350 ml/12 fl oz chicken stock
50 g/2 oz walnut halves, lightly
  toasted and chopped
2 tbsp each freshly chopped mint
  and parsley
salt and freshly ground black pepper

To garnish:

fresh herbs
orange wedges

1 Preheat the oven to 180°C/350°F/Gas Mark 4. To make the stuffing, place the port, raisins and apricots in a bowl and leave for 15 minutes. Heat the oil in a large saucepan. Add the onion and celery and cook for 3–4 minutes. Add the garlic, mixed spice, herbs and chestnuts and cook for 4 minutes, stirring occasionally. Add the rice, half the orange rind and juice and the stock. Simmer for 5 minutes until most liquid is absorbed.

2 Drain the raisins and apricots, reserving the port. Stir into the rice with the walnuts, mint, parsley and seasoning and cook for 2 minutes. Remove and cool.

3 Rinse the poussin cavities, pat dry and season with salt and pepper. Lightly fill the cavities with the stuffing. Tie the legs of together, tucking in the tail. Form any extra stuffing into balls.

4 Place in roasting tins with stuffing balls and brush with melted butter. Drizzle over the remaining butter, remaining orange rind and juice and port. Roast in the preheated oven for 50 minutes or until golden and cooked, basting every 15 minutes. Transfer to a platter, cover with tinfoil and rest. Pour over any pan juices. Garnish with herbs and orange wedges. Serve with the stuffing.

2

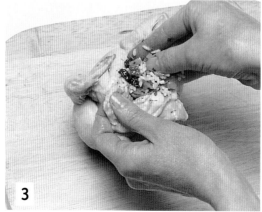
3

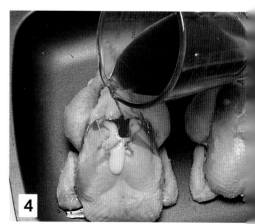
4

Duck with Berry Sauce

INGREDIENTS

Serves 4

4 x 175 g/6 oz boneless duck breasts
salt and freshly ground black pepper
1 tsp sunflower oil

For the sauce:

juice of 1 orange
1 bay leaf
3 tbsp redcurrant jelly
150 g/5 oz fresh or frozen
   mixed berries
2 tbsp dried cranberries or cherries
½ tsp soft light brown sugar
1 tbsp balsamic vinegar
1 tsp freshly chopped mint
sprigs of fresh mint, to garnish

To serve:

freshly cooked potatoes
freshly cooked green beans

1 Remove the skins from the duck breasts and season with a little salt and pepper. Brush a griddle pan with the oil, then heat on the stove until smoking hot.

2 Place the duck, skinned-side down in the pan. Cook over a medium-high heat for 5 minutes, or until well browned. Turn the duck and cook for 2 minutes. Lower the heat and cook for a further 5–8 minutes, or until cooked, but still slightly pink in the centre. Remove from the pan and keep warm.

3 While the duck is cooking, make the sauce. Put the orange juice, bay leaf, redcurrant jelly, fresh or frozen and dried berries and sugar in a small griddle pan. Add any juices left in the griddle pan to the small pan. Slowly bring to the boil, lower the heat and simmer uncovered for 4–5 minutes, until the fruit is soft.

4 Remove the bay leaf. Stir in the vinegar and chopped mint and season to taste with salt and pepper.

5 Slice the duck breasts on the diagonal and arrange on serving plates. Spoon over the berry sauce and garnish with sprigs of fresh mint. Serve immediately with the potatoes and green beans.

HELPFUL HINT

Duck breasts are best served slightly pink in the middle. Whole ducks, however, should be thoroughly cooked.

Guinea Fowl with Calvados & Apples

INGREDIENTS

Serves 4

4 guinea fowl supremes, each about
  150 g/5 oz, skinned
1 tbsp plain flour
1 tbsp sunflower oil
1 onion, peeled and finely sliced
1 garlic clove, peeled and crushed
1 tsp freshly chopped thyme
150 ml/¼ pint dry cider
salt and freshly ground black pepper
3 tbsp Calvados brandy
sprigs of fresh thyme, to garnish

For the caramelised apples:

15 g/½ oz unsalted butter
2 red-skinned eating apples,
  quartered, cored and sliced
1 tsp caster sugar

1 Lightly dust the guinea fowl supremes with the flour.

2 Heat 2 teaspoons of the oil in a large non-stick frying pan and cook the supremes for 2–3 minutes on each side until browned. Remove from the pan and reserve.

3 Heat the remaining teaspoon of oil in the pan and add the onion and garlic. Cook over a medium heat for 10 minutes, stirring occasionally until soft and just beginning to colour.

4 Stir in the chopped thyme and cider. Return the guinea fowl to the pan, season with salt and pepper and bring to a very gentle simmer. Cover and cook over a low heat for 15–20 minutes or until the guinea fowl is tender.

5 Remove the guinea fowl and keep warm. Turn up the heat and boil the sauce until thickened and reduced by half.

6 Meanwhile, prepare the caramelised apples. Melt the butter in a small non-stick pan, add the apple slices in a single layer and sprinkle with the sugar. Cook until the apples are tender and beginning to caramelise, turning once.

7 Put the Calvados in a metal ladle or small saucepan and gently heat until warm. Carefully set alight with a match, let the flames die down, then stir into the sauce.

8 Serve the guinea fowl with the sauce spooned over and garnished with the caramelised apples and sprigs of fresh thyme.

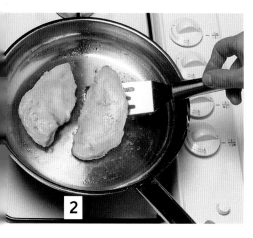
2

4

7

Pheasant with Sage & Blueberries

INGREDIENTS

Serves 4

3 tbsp olive oil

3 shallots, peeled and coarsely
chopped

2 sprigs of fresh sage, coarsely
chopped

1 bay leaf

1 lemon, halved

salt and freshly ground black pepper

2 pheasants or guinea fowl, rinsed
and dried

125 g/4 oz blueberries

4 slices Parma ham or bacon

125 ml/4 fl oz vermouth or
dry white wine

200 ml/⅓ pint chicken stock

3 tbsp double cream
or butter (optional)

1 tbsp brandy

roast potatoes, to serve

1. Preheat oven to 180°C/350°F/Gas Mark 4, 10 minutes before cooking. Place the oil, shallots, sage and bay leaf in a bowl, with the juice from the lemon halves. Season with salt and pepper. Tuck each of the squeezed lemon halves into the birds with 75 g/3 oz of the blueberries, then rub the birds with the marinade and leave for 2–3 hours, basting occasionally.

2. Remove the birds from the marinade and cover each with 2 slices of Parma ham. Tie the legs of each bird with string and place in a roasting tin. Pour over the marinade and add the vermouth. Roast in the preheated oven for 1 hour, or until tender and golden and the juices run clear when a thigh is pierced with a sharp knife or skewer.

3. Transfer to a warm serving plate, cover with tinfoil and discard the string. Skim off any surface fat from the tin and set over a medium-high heat.

4. Add the stock to the tin and bring to the boil, scraping any browned bits from the bottom. Boil until slightly reduced. Whisk in the cream or butter, if using, and simmer until thickened, whisking constantly. Stir in the brandy and strain into a gravy jug. Add the remaining blueberries and keep warm.

5. Using a sharp carving knife, cut each of the birds in half and arrange on the plate with the crispy Parma ham. Serve immediately with roast potatoes and the gravy.

1

2

5

Marinated Pheasant Breasts with Grilled Polenta

INGREDIENTS

Serves 4

3 tbsp extra virgin olive oil
1 tbsp freshly chopped rosemary or
  sage leaves
½ tsp ground cinnamon
grated zest of 1 orange
salt and freshly ground black pepper
8 pheasant or wood pigeon breasts
600 ml/1 pint water
125 g/4 oz quick-cook polenta
2 tbsp butter, diced
40 g/1½ oz Parmesan cheese, grated
1–2 tbsp freshly chopped parsley
assorted salad leaves, to serve

1 Preheat grill just before cooking. Blend 2 tablespoons of the olive oil with the chopped rosemary or sage, cinnamon and orange zest and season to taste with salt and pepper.

2 Place the pheasant breasts in a large, shallow dish, pour over the oil and marinate until required, turning occasionally.

3 Bring the water and 1 teaspoon of salt to the boil in a large, heavy-based saucepan. Slowly whisk in the polenta in a thin, steady stream. Reduce the heat and simmer for 5–10 minutes, or until very thick, stirring constantly.

4 Stir the butter and cheese into the polenta, the parsley and a little black pepper.

5 Turn the polenta out on to a lightly oiled, non-stick baking tray and spread into an even layer about 2 cm/¾ inch thick. Leave to cool, then chill in the refrigerator for about 1 hour, or until the polenta is chilled.

6 Turn the cold polenta on to a work surface. Cut into 10 cm/4 inch squares. Brush with olive oil and arrange on a grill rack. Grill for 2–3 minutes on each side until crisp and golden, then cut each square into triangles and keep warm.

7 Transfer the marinated pheasant breasts to the grill rack and grill for 5 minutes, or until crisp and beginning to colour, turning once. Serve the pheasants immediately with the polenta triangles and salad leaves.

3

4

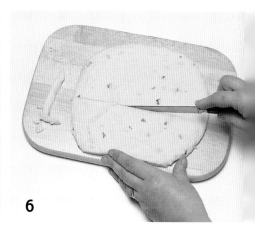
6

Poached Chicken with Salsa Verde Herb Sauce

INGREDIENTS

Serves 6

6 boneless chicken breasts, each
about 175 g/6 oz
600 ml/1 pint chicken stock,
preferably homemade

For the salsa verde:

2 garlic cloves, peeled and chopped
4 tbsp freshly chopped parsley
3 tbsp freshly chopped mint
2 tsp capers
2 tbsp chopped gherkins (optional)
2–3 anchovy fillets in olive oil, drained
and finely chopped (optional)
1 handful wild rocket leaves,
chopped (optional)
2 tbsp lemon juice or red wine vinegar
125 ml/4 fl oz extra virgin olive oil
salt and freshly ground black pepper
sprigs of mint, to garnish
freshly cooked vegetables, to serve

1 Place the chicken breasts with the stock in a large frying pan and bring to the boil. Reduce the heat and simmer for 10–15 minutes, or until cooked. Leave to cool in the stock.

2 To make the salsa verde, switch the motor on a food processor, then drop in the garlic cloves and chop finely. Add the parsley and mint and, using the pulse button, pulse 2–3 times. Add the capers and, if using, add the gherkins, anchovies and rocket. Pulse 2–3 times until the sauce is evenly textured.

3 With the machine still running, pour in the lemon juice or red wine vinegar, then add the olive oil in a slow, steady stream until the sauce is smooth. Season to taste with salt and pepper, then transfer to a large serving bowl and reserve.

4 Carve each chicken breast into thick slices and arrange on serving plates, fanning out the slices slightly. Spoon over a little of the salsa verde on to each chicken breast, garnish with sprigs of mint and serve immediately with freshly cooked vegetables.

1

3

4

Chicken & Asparagus with Tagliatelle

INGREDIENTS

Serves 4

275 g/10 oz fresh asparagus

50 g/2 oz butter

4 spring onions, trimmed and coarsely chopped

350 g/12 oz boneless, skinless chicken breast, thinly sliced

2 tbsp white vermouth

300 ml/½ pint double cream

2 tbsp freshly chopped chives

400 g/14 oz fresh tagliatelle

50 g/2 oz Parmesan or pecorino cheese, grated

snipped chives, to garnish

extra Parmesan cheese (optional), to serve

1 Using a swivel-bladed vegetable peeler, lightly peel the asparagus stalks and then cook in lightly salted, boiling water for 2–3 minutes, or until just tender. Drain and refresh in cold water, then cut into 4 cm/1½ inch pieces and reserve.

2 Melt the butter in a large frying pan then add the spring onions and the chicken and fry for 4 minutes. Add the vermouth and allow to reduce until the liquid has evaporated. Pour in the cream and half the chives. Cook gently for 5–7 minutes, until the sauce has thickened and slightly reduced and the chicken is tender.

3 Bring a large saucepan of lightly salted water to the boil and cook the tagliatelle for 4–5 minutes, or until 'al dente'. Drain and immediately add to the chicken and cream sauce.

4 Using a pair of spaghetti tongs or kitchen forks, lightly toss the sauce and pasta until it is mixed thoroughly. Add the remaining chives and the Parmesan cheese and toss gently. Garnish with snipped chives and serve immediately, with extra Parmesan cheese, if desired.

TASTY TIP

Freshly made pasta will cook in 30–60 seconds. It is cooked when it rises to the surface. Bought fresh pasta will take between 2–3 minutes. Dried pasta takes longer to cook (between 4–10 minutes) depending on the variety – check the packet instructions.

2

3

4

Herbed Hasselback Potatoes with Roast Chicken

INGREDIENTS

Serves 4

8 medium, evenly-sized
  potatoes, peeled
3 large sprigs of fresh rosemary
1 tbsp oil
salt and freshly ground black pepper
350 g/12 oz baby parsnips, peeled
350 g/12 oz baby carrots, peeled
350 g/12 oz baby leeks, trimmed
75 g/3 oz butter
finely grated rind of 1 lemon,
  preferably unwaxed
1.6 kg/3½ lb chicken

FOOD FACT

Hasselback potatoes were named after the Stockholm restaurant of the same name. Using chopsticks is a great way of ensuring that you slice just far enough through the potatoes so that they fan out during cooking. The potatoes can be given an attractive golden finish by mixing ¼ tsp ground turmeric or paprika with the oil.

1 Preheat the oven to 200°C/400°F/Gas Mark 6, about 15 minutes before cooking. Place a chopstick on either side of a potato and, with a sharp knife, cut down through the potato until you reach the chopsticks; take care not to cut right through the potato. Repeat these cuts every 5 mm/¼ inch along the length of the potato. Carefully ease 2–4 of the slices apart and slip in a few rosemary sprigs. Repeat with remaining potatoes. Brush with the oil and season well with salt and pepper.

2 Place the seasoned potatoes in a large roasting tin. Add the parsnips, carrots and leeks to the potatoes in the tin, cover with a wire rack or trivet.

3 Beat the butter and lemon rind together and season to taste. Smear the chicken with the lemon butter and place on the rack over the vegetables.

4 Roast in the preheated oven for 1 hour 40 minutes, basting the chicken and vegetables occasionally, until cooked thoroughly. The juices should run clear when the thigh is pierced with a skewer. Place the cooked chicken on a warmed serving platter, arrange the roast vegetables around it and serve immediately.

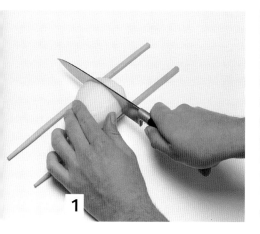

1

1

3

Mexican Chicken

INGREDIENTS

Serves 4

1.4 kg/3 lb oven-ready
   chicken, jointed
3 tbsp plain flour
½ tsp ground paprika pepper
salt and freshly ground black pepper
2 tsp sunflower oil
1 small onion, peeled and chopped
1 red chilli, deseeded and
   finely chopped
½ tsp ground cumin
½ tsp dried oregano
300 ml/½ pint chicken or
   vegetable stock
1 green pepper, deseeded and sliced
2 tsp cocoa powder
1 tbsp lime juice
2 tsp clear honey
3 tbsp Greek yogurt

To garnish:
sliced limes
red chilli slices
sprig of fresh oregano

To serve:
freshly cooked rice
fresh green salad leaves

1   Using a knife, remove the skin from the chicken joints.

2   In a shallow dish, mix together the flour, paprika, salt and pepper. Coat the chicken on both sides with flour and shake off any excess if necessary.

3   Heat the oil in a large non-stick frying pan. Add the chicken and brown on both sides. Transfer to a plate and reserve.

4   Add the onion and red chilli to the pan and gently cook for 5 minutes, or until the onion is soft. Stir occasionally.

5   Stir in the cumin and oregano and cook for a further minute. Pour in the stock and bring to the boil.

6   Return the chicken to the pan, cover and cook for 40 minutes. Add the green pepper and cook for 10 minutes, until the chicken is cooked. Remove the chicken and pepper with a slotted spoon and keep warm in a serving dish.

7   Blend the cocoa powder with 1 tablespoon of warm water. Stir into the sauce, then boil rapidly until the sauce has thickened and reduced by about one third. Stir in the lime juice, honey and yogurt.

8   Pour the sauce over the chicken and pepper and garnish with the lime slices, chilli and oregano. Serve immediately with the freshly cooked rice and green salad.

2

5

7

Turkey Escalopes Marsala with Wilted Watercress

INGREDIENTS

Serves 4

4 turkey escalopes, each about
  150 g/5 oz
25 g/1 oz plain flour
½ tsp dried thyme
salt and freshly ground black pepper
1–2 tbsp olive oil
125 g/4 oz watercress
40 g/1½ oz butter
225 g/8 oz mushrooms, wiped
  and quartered
50 ml/2 fl oz dry Marsala wine
50 ml/2 fl oz chicken stock or water

1 Place each turkey escalope between 2 sheets of non-stick baking parchment and, using a meat mallet or rolling pin, pound to make an escalope about 3 mm/⅛ inch thick. Put the flour in a shallow dish, add the thyme, season to taste with salt and pepper then coat each escalope lightly with the flour mixture, and reserve.

2 Heat the olive oil in a large frying pan, then add the watercress and stir-fry for about 2 minutes, until just wilted and brightly coloured. Season with salt and pepper. Using a slotted spoon, transfer the watercress to a plate and keep warm.

3 Add half the butter to the frying pan and when melted, add the mushrooms. Stir-fry for 4 minutes, or until golden and tender. Remove from the pan and reserve.

4 Add the remaining butter to the pan and, working in batches if necessary, cook the flour-coated escalopes for 2–3 minutes on each side, or until golden and cooked thoroughly, adding the remaining oil, if necessary. Remove from the pan and keep warm.

5 Add the Marsala wine to the pan and stir, scraping up any browned bits from the bottom of the pan. Add the stock or water and bring to the boil over a high heat. Season lightly.

6 Return the escalopes and mushrooms to the pan and reheat gently until piping hot. Divide the warm watercress between four plates. Arrange 1 escalope over each serving of wilted watercress and spoon over the mushrooms and Marsala sauce. Serve immediately.

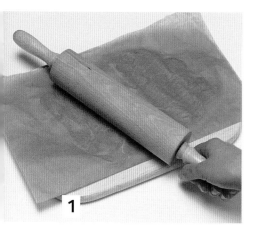
1

2

4

Chicken & White Wine Risotto

INGREDIENTS

Serves 4–6

2 tbsp oil

125 g/4 oz unsalted butter

2 shallots, peeled and finely chopped

300 g/11 oz Arborio rice

600 ml/1 pint dry white wine

750 ml/1¼ pints chicken stock, heated

350 g/12 oz skinless chicken breast fillets, thinly sliced

50 g/2 oz Parmesan cheese, grated

2 tbsp freshly chopped dill or parsley

salt and freshly ground black pepper

HELPFUL HINT

Keep the stock to be added to the risotto at a low simmer in a separate saucepan, so that it is piping hot when added to the rice. This will ensure that the dish is kept at a constant heat during cooking, which is important to achieve a perfect creamy texture.

1 Heat the oil and half the butter in a large heavy-based saucepan over a medium-high heat. Add the shallots and cook for 2 minutes, or until softened, stirring frequently. Add the rice and cook for 2–3 minutes, stirring frequently, until the rice is translucent and well coated.

2 Pour in half the wine; it will bubble and steam rapidly. Cook, stirring constantly, until the liquid is absorbed. Add a ladleful of the hot stock and cook until the liquid is absorbed. Carefully stir in the chicken.

3 Continue adding the stock, about half a ladleful at a time, allowing each addition to be absorbed before adding the next; never allow the rice to cook dry. This process should take about 20 minutes. The risotto should have a creamy consistency and the rice should be tender, but firm to the bite.

4 Stir in the remaining wine and cook for 2–3 minutes. Remove from the heat and stir in the remaining butter with the Parmesan cheese and half the chopped herbs. Season to taste with salt and pepper. Spoon into warmed shallow bowls and sprinkle each with the remaining chopped herbs. Serve immediately.

2

3

4

Chicken with Porcini Mushrooms

INGREDIENTS

Serves 4

2 tbsp olive oil

4 boneless chicken breasts,
  preferably free range

2 garlic cloves, peeled and crushed

150 ml/ ¼ pint dry vermouth or dry
  white wine

salt and freshly ground black pepper

25 g/1 oz butter

450 g/1 lb porcini or wild
  mushrooms, thickly sliced

1 tbsp freshly chopped oregano

sprigs of fresh basil, to
  garnish (optional)

freshly cooked rice, to serve

TASTY TIP

Porcini or cep mushrooms grow wild and are relatively easy to find, if you know where to look. They can, however, be very expensive to buy fresh. If they are unavailable, substitute with fresh button or chestnut mushrooms and 15 g/½ oz reconstituted dried porcini instead.

1 Heat the olive oil in a large, heavy-based frying pan, then add the chicken breasts, skin-side down and cook for about 10 minutes, or until they are well browned. Remove the chicken breasts and reserve. Add the garlic, stir into the juices and cook for 1 minute.

2 Pour the vermouth or white wine into the pan and season to taste with salt and pepper. Return the chicken to the pan. Bring to the boil, reduce the heat to low and simmer for about 20 minutes, or until tender.

3 In another large frying pan, heat the butter and add the sliced porcini or wild mushrooms. Stir-fry for about 5 minutes, or until the mushrooms are golden and tender.

4 Add the porcini or wild mushrooms and any juices to the chicken. Season to taste, then add the chopped oregano. Stir together gently and cook for 1 minute longer. Transfer to a large serving plate and garnish with sprigs of fresh basil, if desired. Serve immediately with rice.

Braised Chicken with Aubergine

INGREDIENTS

Serves 4

3 tbsp vegetable oil

12 chicken thighs

2 large aubergines, trimmed
   and cubed

4 garlic cloves, peeled and crushed

2 tsp freshly grated root ginger

900 ml/1½ pints vegetable stock

2 tbsp light soy sauce

2 tbsp Chinese preserved black beans

6 spring onions, trimmed and thinly
   sliced diagonally

1 tbsp cornflour

1 tbsp sesame oil

spring onion tassels, to garnish

freshly cooked noodles or rice

TASTY TIP

To make your own Chinese-style vegetable stock, roughly chop 1 onion, 2 celery sticks and 2 carrots and place in a large saucepan with a few dried shiitake mushrooms and slices of fresh root ginger. Pour in 1.4 litres/2½ pints cold water, bring to the boil, partially cover and simmer for 30 minutes. Leave to cool, then strain through a fine sieve. Refrigerate.

1 Heat a wok or large frying pan, add the oil and when hot, add the chicken thighs and cook over a medium high heat for 5 minutes, or until browned all over. Transfer to a large plate and keep warm.

2 Add the aubergine to the wok and cook over a high heat for 5 minutes or until browned, turning occasionally. Add the garlic and ginger and stir-fry for 1 minute.

3 Return the chicken to the wok, pour in the stock and add the soy sauce and black beans. Bring to the boil, then simmer for 20 minutes, or until the chicken is tender. Add the spring onions after 10 minutes.

4 Blend the cornflour with 2 tablespoons of water. Stir into the wok and simmer until the sauce has thickened. Stir in the sesame oil, heat for 30 seconds, then remove from the heat. Garnish with spring onion tassels and serve immediately with noodles or rice.

Pheasant with Portabella Mushrooms & Red Wine Gravy

INGREDIENTS

Serves 4

25 g/1 oz butter

1 tbsp olive oil

2 small pheasants (preferably hens)
   rinsed, well dried and halved

8 shallots, peeled

300 g/11 oz portabella mushrooms,
   thickly sliced

2–3 sprigs of fresh thyme or
   rosemary, leaves stripped

300 ml/½ pint Valpolicella or fruity
   red wine

300 ml/½ pint hot chicken stock

1 tbsp cornflour

2 tbsp balsamic vinegar

2 tbsp redcurrant jelly, or to taste

2 tbsp freshly chopped flat-leaf parsley

salt and freshly ground black pepper

sprigs of fresh thyme, to garnish

1 Preheat oven to 180°C/350°F/Gas Mark 4. Heat the butter and oil in a large saucepan or frying pan. Add the pheasant halves and shallots working in batches, if necessary, and cook for 10 minutes, or until golden on all sides, shaking the pan to glaze the shallots. Transfer to a casserole dish large enough to hold the pieces in a single layer. Add the mushroom and thyme to the pan and cook for 2–3 minutes, or until beginning to colour. Transfer to the dish with the pheasant halves.

2 Add the wine to the saucepan; it will bubble and steam. Cook, stirring up any browned bits from the pan and allow to reduce by half. Pour in the stock and bring to the boil, then pour over the pheasant halves. Cover and braise in the preheated oven for 50 minutes, or until tender. Remove the pheasant halves and vegetables to a wide, shallow serving dish and set the casserole or roasting tin over a medium-high heat.

3 Skim off any surface fat and bring to the boil. Blend the cornflour with the vinegar and stir into the sauce with the redcurrant jelly. Boil until the sauce is reduced and thickened slightly. Stir in the parsley and season to taste with salt and pepper. Pour over the pheasant halves, garnish with sprigs of fresh thyme and serve immediately.

1

1

3

Aromatic Chicken Curry

INGREDIENTS

Serves 4

125 g/4 oz red lentils

2 tsp ground coriander

½ tsp cumin seeds

2 tsp mild curry paste

1 bay leaf

small strip of lemon rind

600 ml/1 pint chicken or
  vegetable stock

8 chicken thighs, skinned

175 g/6 oz spinach leaves, rinsed
  and shredded

1 tbsp freshly chopped coriander

2 tsp lemon juice

salt and freshly ground black pepper

To serve:

freshly cooked rice

low fat natural yogurt

HELPFUL HINT

Dry-frying spices really releases their flavour. It is a particularly good way to flavour lean meat or fish. Try mixing dry-fried spices with a little water or oil to make a paste. Spread the paste on meat or fish before baking to make a spicy crust.

1 Put the lentils in a sieve and rinse thoroughly under cold running water.

2 Dry-fry the ground coriander and cumin seeds in a large saucepan over a low heat for about 30 seconds. Stir in the curry paste.

3 Add the lentils to the saucepan with the bay leaf and lemon rind, then pour in the stock.

4 Stir, then slowly bring to the boil. Turn down the heat, half-cover the pan with a lid and simmer gently for 5 minutes, stirring occasionally.

5 Secure the chicken thighs with cocktail sticks to keep their shape. Place in the pan and half-cover. Simmer for 15 minutes.

6 Stir in the shredded spinach and cook for a further 25 minutes or until the chicken is very tender and the sauce is thick.

7 Remove the bay leaf and lemon rind. Stir in the coriander and lemon juice, then season to taste with salt and pepper. Serve immediately with the rice and a little natural yogurt.

3

5

6

Sauvignon Chicken & Mushroom Filo Pie

INGREDIENTS

Serves 4

1 onion, peeled and chopped
1 leek, trimmed and chopped
225 ml/8 fl oz chicken stock
3 x 175 g/6 oz chicken breasts
150 ml/¼ pint dry white wine
1 bay leaf
175 g/6 oz baby button mushrooms
2 tbsp plain flour
1 tbsp freshly chopped tarragon
salt and freshly ground black pepper
sprig of fresh parsley, to garnish
seasonal vegetables, to serve

For the topping:

75 g/3 oz (about 5 sheets) filo pastry
1 tbsp sunflower oil
1 tsp sesame seeds

1. Preheat the oven to 190°C/375°F/Gas Mark 5. Put the onion and leek in a heavy-based saucepan with 125 ml/4 fl oz of the stock.

2. Bring to the boil, cover and simmer for 5 minutes, then uncover and cook until all the stock has evaporated and the vegetables are tender.

3. Cut the chicken into bite-sized cubes. Add to the pan with the remaining stock, wine and bay leaf. Cover and gently simmer for 5 minutes. Add the mushrooms and simmer for a further 5 minutes.

4. Blend the flour with 3 tablespoons of cold water. Stir into the pan and cook, stirring all the time until the sauce has thickened.

5. Stir the tarragon into the sauce and season with salt and pepper.

6. Spoon the mixture into a 1.2 litre/2 pint pie dish, discarding the bay leaf.

7. Lightly brush a sheet of filo pastry with a little of the oil.

8. Crumple the pastry slightly. Arrange on top of the filling. Repeat with the remaining filo sheets and oil, then sprinkle the top of the pie with the sesame seeds.

9. Bake the pie on the middle shelf of the preheated oven for 20 minutes until the filo pastry topping is golden and crisp. Garnish with a sprig of parsley. Serve the pie immediately with the seasonal vegetables.

3

6

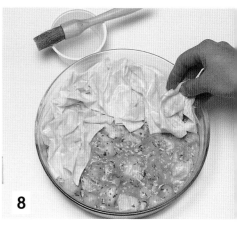
8

Chicken & Seafood Risotto

INGREDIENTS

Serves 6–8

125 ml/4 fl oz olive oil

1.4 kg/3 lb chicken, cut into 8 pieces

350 g/12 oz spicy chorizo sausage,
   cut into 1 cm/½ inch pieces

125 g/4 oz cured ham, diced

1 onion, peeled and chopped

2 red or yellow peppers, deseeded
   and cut into 2.5 cm/1 inch pieces

4 garlic cloves, peeled and
   finely chopped

750 g/1 lb 10 oz short-grain Spanish
   rice or Arborio rice

2 bay leaves

1 tsp dried thyme

1 tsp saffron strands, lightly crushed

200 ml/7 fl oz dry white wine

1.6 litres/2¾ pints chicken stock

salt and freshly ground black pepper

125 g/4 oz fresh shelled peas

450 g/1 lb uncooked prawns

36 clams and/or mussels, well
   scrubbed

2 tbsp freshly chopped parsley

To garnish:

lemon wedges

fresh parsley sprigs

1 Heat half the oil in a 45.5 cm/18 inch paella pan or deep wide frying pan. Add the chicken pieces and fry for 15 minutes, turning constantly, until golden. Remove from the pan and reserve. Add the chorizo and ham to the pan and cook for 6 minutes until crisp, stirring occasionally. Remove and add to the chicken.

2 Add the onion to the pan and cook for 3 minutes, or until beginning to soften. Add the peppers and garlic and cook for 2 minutes; add to the reserved chicken, chorizo and ham.

3 Add the remaining oil to the pan and stir in the rice until well coated. Stir in the bay leaves, thyme and saffron, then pour in the wine and bubble until evaporated, stirring and scraping up any bits on the bottom of the pan. Stir in the stock and bring to the boil, stirring occasionally.

4 Return the chicken, chorizo, ham and vegetables to the pan, burying them gently in the rice. Season to taste with salt and pepper. Reduce the heat and simmer for 10 minutes, stirring occasionally.

5 Add the peas and seafood, pushing them gently into the rice. Cover, cook over a low heat for 5 minutes, or until the rice and prawns are tender and the clams and mussels open (discard any that do not open). Stand for 5 minutes. Sprinkle with the parsley, garnish and serve.

1

3

5

Chicken & Summer Vegetable Risotto

INGREDIENTS

Serves 4

1 litre/1¾ pint chicken or
  vegetable stock
225 g/8 oz baby asparagus spears
125 g/4 oz French beans
15 g/½ oz butter
1 small onion, peeled and
  finely chopped
150 ml/¼ pint dry white wine
275 g/10 oz arborio rice
pinch of saffron strands
75 g/3 oz frozen peas, thawed
225 g/8 oz cooked chicken, skinned
  and diced
juice of ½ lemon
salt and freshly ground black pepper
25 g/1 oz Parmesan, shaved

1   Bring the stock to the boil in a large saucepan. Trim the asparagus and cut into 4 cm/1½ inch lengths.

2   Blanch the asparagus in the stock for 1–2 minutes or until tender, then remove with a slotted spoon and reserve.

3   Halve the green beans and cook in the boiling stock for 4 minutes. Remove and reserve. Turn down the heat and keep the stock barely simmering.

4   Melt the butter in a heavy-based saucepan. Add the onion and cook gently for about 5 minutes.

5   Pour the wine into the pan and boil rapidly until the liquid has almost reduced. Add the rice and cook, stirring for 1 minute until the grains are coated and look translucent.

6   Add the saffron and a ladle of the stock. Simmer, stirring all the time, until the stock has absorbed. Continue adding the stock, a ladle at a time, until it has all been absorbed.

7   After 15 minutes the risotto should be creamy with a slight bite to it. If not add a little more stock and cook for a few more minutes, or until it is of the correct texture and consistency.

8   Add the peas, reserved vegetables, chicken and lemon juice. Season to taste with salt and pepper and cook for 3–4 minutes or until the chicken is thoroughly heated and piping hot.

9   Spoon the risotto on to warmed serving plates. Scatter each portion with a few shavings of Parmesan cheese and serve immediately.

2

5

6

Creamy Chicken Cannelloni

INGREDIENTS

Serves 6

50 g/2 oz butter

2 garlic cloves, peeled and
  finely crushed

225 g/8 oz button mushrooms,
  thinly sliced

2 tbsp freshly chopped basil

450 g/1 lb fresh spinach, blanched

salt and freshly ground black pepper

2 tbsp plain flour

300 ml/½ pint chicken stock

150 ml/¼ pint dry white wine

150 ml/¼ pint double cream

350 g/12 oz skinless, boneless,
  cooked chicken, chopped

175 g/6 oz Parma ham,
  finely chopped

½ tsp dried thyme

225 g/8 oz precooked
  cannelloni tubes

175 g/6 oz Gruyère cheese, grated

40 g/1½ oz Parmesan cheese, grated

sprig of fresh basil, to garnish

1 Preheat oven to 190°C/375°F/Gas Mark 5, 10 minutes before cooking. Lightly butter a 28 x 23 cm/11 x 9 inch ovenproof baking dish. Heat half the butter in a large heavy-based frying pan, then add the garlic and mushrooms and cook gently for 5 minutes. Stir in the basil and the spinach and cook, covered, until the spinach is wilted and just tender, stirring frequently. Season to taste with salt and pepper, then spoon into the dish and reserve.

2 Melt the remaining butter in a small saucepan, then stir in the flour and cook for about 2 minutes, stirring constantly. Remove from the heat, stir in the stock, then the wine and the cream. Return to the heat, bring to the boil and simmer, until the sauce is thick and smooth, then season to taste.

3 Measure 125 ml/4 fl oz of the cream sauce into a bowl. Add the chopped chicken, Parma ham and the dried thyme. Season to taste, then spoon the chicken mixture into the cannelloni tubes, arranging them in 2 long rows on top of the spinach layer.

4 Add half the Gruyère cheese to the cream sauce and heat, stirring, until the cheese melts. Pour over the sauce and top with the remaining Gruyère and Parmesan cheeses. Bake in the preheated oven for 35 minutes, or until golden and bubbling. Garnish with a sprig of fresh basil and serve immediately.

1

2

3

Chicken Liver & Tomato Sauce with Tagliolini

INGREDIENTS

Serves 4

50 ml/2 fl oz extra virgin olive oil

1 onion, peeled and finely chopped

2 garlic cloves, peeled and
   finely chopped

125 ml/4 fl oz dry red wine

2 x 400 g cans Italian peeled plum
   tomatoes with juice

1 tbsp tomato purée

1 tbsp freshly chopped sage or
   thyme leaves

salt and freshly ground black pepper

350 g/12 oz fresh or dried tagliolini,
   papardelle or tagliatelle

25 g/1 oz butter

225 g/8 oz fresh chicken livers,
   trimmed and cut in half

plain flour for dusting

sprigs of fresh sage,
   to garnish (optional)

1 Heat half the olive oil in a large, deep, heavy-based frying pan and add the onion. Cook, stirring frequently, for 4–5 minutes, or until soft and translucent. Stir in the garlic and cook for a further minute.

2 Add the red wine and cook, stirring until the wine is reduced by half, then add the tomatoes, tomato purée and half the sage or thyme. Bring to the boil, stirring to break up the tomatoes. Simmer for 30 minutes, stirring occasionally, or until the sauce has reduced and thickened. Season to taste with salt and pepper.

3 Bring a large saucepan of lightly salted water to the boil. Add the pasta and cook for 7–10 minutes, or until 'al dente'.

4 Meanwhile, in a large heavy-based frying pan, melt the remaining oil and the butter and heat until very hot. Pat the chicken livers dry and dust lightly with a little flour. Add to the pan, a few at a time, and cook for 5 minutes, or until crisp and browned, turning carefully – the livers should still be pink inside.

5 Drain the pasta well and turn into a large, warmed serving bowl. Stir the livers carefully into the tomato sauce, then pour the sauce over the drained pasta and toss gently to coat. Garnish with a sprig of fresh sage and serve immediately.

2

2

4

Chicken Pie with Sweet Potato Topping

INGREDIENTS

Serves 4

700 g/1½ lb sweet potatoes, peeled
  and cut into chunks
salt and freshly ground black pepper
250 g/9 oz potatoes, peeled and cut
  into chunks
150 ml/¼ pint milk
25 g/1 oz butter
2 tsp brown sugar
grated rind of 1 orange
4 skinless chicken breast fillets, diced
1 medium onion, peeled and
  coarsely chopped
125 g/4 oz baby mushrooms,
  stems trimmed
2 leeks, trimmed and thickly sliced
150 ml/¼ pint dry white wine
1 chicken stock cube
1 tbsp freshly chopped parsley
50 ml/2 fl oz crème fraîche or thick
  double cream
green vegetables, to serve

1 Preheat the oven to 190°C/375°F/Gas Mark 5, 10 minutes before required. Cook the potatoes in lightly salted boiling water until tender. Drain well, then return to the saucepan and mash until smooth and creamy, gradually adding the milk, then the butter, sugar and orange rind. Season to taste with salt and pepper and reserve.

2 Place the chicken in a saucepan with the onion, mushrooms, leeks, wine, stock cube and season to taste. Simmer, covered, until the chicken and vegetables are tender. Using a slotted spoon, transfer the chicken and vegetables to a 1.1 litre/2 pint pie dish. Add the parsley and crème fraîche or cream to the liquid in the pan and bring to the boil. Simmer until thickened and smooth, stirring constantly. Pour over the chicken in the pie dish, mix and cool.

3 Spread the mashed potato over the chicken filling, and swirl the surface into decorative peaks. Bake in the preheated oven for 35 minutes, or until the top is golden and the chicken filling is heated through. Serve immediately with fresh green vegetables.

Chicken Under a Brick

INGREDIENTS

Serves 4–6

1.8 kg/4 lb free range corn-fed,
  oven-ready chicken
50 ml/2 fl oz olive oil
sea salt and freshly ground
  black pepper

To garnish:
sprigs of fresh basil
chives
tossed bitter salad leaves, to serve

1 Rinse the chicken and dry well, inside and out. Using poultry shears or kitchen scissors, cut along each side of the backbone of the chicken and discard or use for stock. Place the chicken skin-side up on a work surface and, using the palm of your hand, press down firmly to break the breast bone and flatten the bird.

2 Turn the chicken breast-side up and use a sharp knife to slit the skin between the breast and thigh on each side. Fold the legs in and push the drumstick bones through the slits. Tuck the wing under, the chicken should be as flat as possible.

3 Heat the olive oil in a large, heavy-based frying pan until very hot, but not smoking. Place the chicken in the pan, skin-side down, and place a flat lid or plate directly on top of the chicken. Top with a brick (hence the name) or 2 kg/5 lb weight. Cook for 12–15 minutes, or until golden brown.

4 Remove the weights and lid and, using a pair of tongs, turn the chicken carefully, then season to taste with salt and pepper. Cover and weight the lid again, then cook for 12–15 minutes longer, until the chicken is tender and the juices run clear when a thigh is pierced with a sharp knife or skewer.

5 Transfer the chicken to a serving plate and cover loosely with tinfoil to keep warm. Allow to rest for at least 10 minutes before carving. Garnish with sprigs of basil and chives and serve with salad leaves.

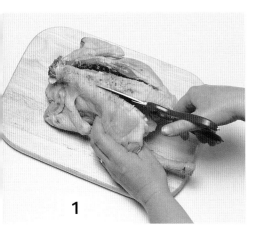

1

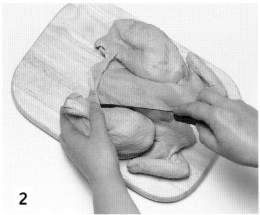

2

3

Chilli Roast Chicken

INGREDIENTS

Serves 4

3 medium-hot fresh red
  chillies, deseeded

1/2 tsp ground turmeric

1 tsp cumin seeds

1 tsp coriander seeds

2 garlic cloves, peeled and crushed

2.5 cm/1 inch piece fresh root ginger,
  peeled and chopped

1 tbsp lemon juice

1 tbsp olive oil

2 tbsp roughly chopped
  fresh coriander

1/2 tsp salt

freshly ground black pepper

1.4 kg/3 lb oven-ready chicken

15 g/1/2 oz unsalted butter, melted

550 g/1 1/4 lb butternut squash

fresh parsley and coriander sprigs,
  to garnish

To serve

4 baked potatoes

seasonal green vegetables

1 Preheat the oven to 190°C/375°F/Gas Mark 5. Roughly chop the chillies and put in a food processor with the turmeric, cumin seeds, coriander seeds, garlic, ginger, lemon juice, olive oil, coriander, salt, pepper and 2 tablespoons of cold water. Blend to a paste, leaving the ingredients still slightly chunky.

2 Starting at the neck end of the chicken, gently ease up the skin to loosen it from the breast. Reserve 3 tablespoons of the paste. Push the remaining paste over the chicken breast under the skin, spreading it evenly.

3 Put the chicken in a large roasting tin. Mix the reserved chilli paste with the melted butter. Use 1 tablespoon to brush evenly over the chicken, roast in the preheated oven for 20 minutes.

4 Meanwhile, halve, peel and scoop out the seeds from the butternut squash. Cut into large chunks and mix in the remaining chilli paste and butter mixture.

5 Arrange the butternut squash around the chicken. Roast for a further hour, basting with the cooking juices about every 20 minutes until the chicken is fully cooked and the squash tender. Garnish with parsley and coriander. Serve hot with baked potatoes and green vegetables.

1

2

4

Creamy Chicken & Rice Pilau

INGREDIENTS

Serves 4–6

350 g/12 oz basmati rice
salt and freshly ground black pepper
50 g/2 oz butter
100 g/3½ oz flaked almonds
75 g/3 oz unsalted shelled
   pistachio nuts
4–6 skinless chicken breast fillets,
   each cut into 4 pieces
2 tbsp vegetable oil
2 medium onions, peeled and
   thinly sliced
2 garlic cloves, peeled and
   finely chopped
2.5 cm/1 inch piece of fresh root
   ginger, finely chopped
6 green cardamom pods,
   lightly crushed
4–6 whole cloves
2 bay leaves
1 tsp ground coriander
½ tsp cayenne pepper, or to taste
225 ml/8 fl oz natural yogurt
225 ml/8 fl oz double cream
225 g/8 oz seedless green grapes,
   halved if large
2 tbsp freshly chopped coriander
   or mint

1 Bring a saucepan of lightly salted water to the boil. Gradually pour in the rice; return to the boil, then simmer for about 12 minutes until tender. Drain, rinse under cold water and reserve.

2 Heat the butter in a large deep frying pan over a medium-high heat. Add the almonds and pistachios and cook for about 2 minutes, stirring constantly, until golden. Using a slotted spoon, transfer to a plate.

3 Add the chicken pieces to the pan and cook for 5 minutes, or until golden, turning once. Remove from the pan and reserve. Add the oil to the pan and cook the onions for 10 minutes, or until golden, stirring frequently. Stir in the garlic, ginger and spices and cook for 2–3 minutes, stirring.

4 Add 2–3 tablespoons of the yogurt and cook, stirring until the moisture evaporates. Continue adding the yogurt in this way until it is used up.

5 Return the chicken and nuts to the pan and stir. Stir in 125 ml/4 fl oz of boiling water and season to taste with salt and pepper. Cook, covered, over a low heat for 10 minutes until the chicken is tender. Stir in the cream, grapes and half the herbs. Gently fold in the rice. Heat through for 5 minutes and sprinkle with the remaining herbs, then serve.

2

3

5

Grilled Spiced Chicken with Tomato & Shallot Chutney

INGREDIENTS

Serves 4

3 tbsp sunflower oil

2 hot red chillies, deseeded
and chopped

3 garlic cloves, peeled and chopped

1 tsp ground turmeric

1 tsp cumin seeds

1 tsp fennel seeds

1 tbsp freshly chopped basil

1 tbsp dark brown sugar

125 ml/4 fl oz rice or white
wine vinegar

2 tsp sesame oil

4 large chicken breast quarters,
wings attached

225 g/8 oz small shallots, peeled
and halved

2 tbsp Chinese rice wine or dry sherry

50 g/2 oz caster sugar

175 g/6 oz cherry tomatoes, halved

2 tbsp light soy sauce

To garnish:

sprigs of fresh coriander
sprigs of fresh dill
lemon wedges

1 Preheat the grill to medium, 5 minutes before cooking. Heat a wok or large frying pan, add 1 tablespoon of the sunflower oil and when hot, add the chillies, garlic, turmeric, cumin, fennel seeds, and basil. Fry for 5 minutes, add the sugar and 2 tablespoons of vinegar and stir until the sugar has dissolved. Remove, stir in the sesame oil and leave to cool.

2 Cut 3 or 4 deep slashes in the thickest part of the chicken breasts. Spread the spice paste over the chicken, place in a dish, cover and marinate in the refrigerator for at least 4 hours or overnight.

3 Heat the remaining sunflower oil in a saucepan, add the shallots and remaining garlic and cook gently for 15 minutes. Add the remaining vinegar, Chinese rice wine or sherry and caster sugar with 50 ml/2 fl oz water. Bring to the boil and simmer rapidly for 10 minutes, or until thickened. Add the tomatoes with the soy sauce. Simmer for 5–10 minutes, or until the liquid is reduced. Leave the chutney to cool.

4 Transfer the chicken pieces to a grill pan and cook under the preheated grill for 15–20 minutes on each side, or until the chicken is cooked through, basting frequently. Garnish with coriander sprigs and lemon wedges and serve immediately with the chutney.

1

2

3

Lemon Chicken Rice

INGREDIENTS

Serves 4

2 tbsp sunflower oil
4 chicken leg portions
1 medium onion, peeled and chopped
1–2 garlic cloves, peeled and crushed
1 tbsp curry powder
25 g/1 oz butter
225 g/8 oz long-grain white rice
1 lemon, preferably unwaxed, sliced
600 ml/1 pint chicken stock
salt and freshly ground black pepper
2 tbsp flaked, toasted almonds
sprigs of fresh coriander, to garnish

TASTY TIP

Choose a strength of curry powder according to personal taste. There is a huge range of brands and mixtures available, from mild korma style through to medium madras or hot vindaloo. Unless you use spices frequently, buy them in small quantities, as they quickly become stale and lose their flavour. Store in clear glass jars in a cool, dark place.

1. Preheat the oven to 180°C/350°F/Gas Mark 4, about 10 minutes before required. Heat the oil in a large frying pan, add the chicken legs and cook, turning, until sealed and golden all over. Using a slotted spoon, remove from the pan and reserve.

2. Add the onion and garlic to the oil remaining in the frying pan and cook for 5–7 minutes, or until just beginning to brown. Sprinkle in the curry powder and cook, stirring, for a further 1 minute. Return the chicken to the pan and stir well, then remove from the heat.

3. Melt the butter in a large heavy-based saucepan. Add the rice and cook, stirring, to ensure that all the grains are coated in the melted butter, then remove from the heat.

4. Stir the lemon slices into the chicken mixture, then spoon the mixture onto the rice and pour over the stock. Season to taste with salt and pepper.

5. Cover with a tight-fitting lid and cook in the preheated oven for 45 minutes, or until the rice is tender and the chicken is cooked thoroughly. Serve sprinkled with the toasted flaked almonds and sprigs of coriander.

Lemon Chicken with Basil & Linguine

INGREDIENTS

Serves 4

grated rind and juice of 1 large lemon

2 garlic cloves, peeled and crushed

2 tbsp basil-flavoured extra virgin
olive oil

4 tbsp freshly chopped basil

salt and freshly ground black pepper

450 g/1 lb skinless, boneless chicken
breast, cut into bite-sized pieces

1 onion, peeled and finely chopped

3 celery stalks, trimmed and
thinly sliced

175 g/6 oz mushrooms, wiped
and halved

2 tbsp plain flour

150 ml/¼ pint white wine

150 ml/¼ pint chicken stock

350–450 g/12 oz–1 lb linguine

To garnish:

lemon zest

fresh basil leaves

1 Blend the lemon rind and juice, garlic, half the oil, half the basil and salt and pepper in a large bowl. Add the chicken pieces and toss well to coat. Allow to stand for about 1 hour, stirring occasionally.

2 Heat the remaining oil in a large non-stick frying pan, then add the sliced onion and cook for 3–4 minutes, or until slightly softened. Using a slotted spoon, drain the chicken pieces and add to the frying pan, reserving the marinade. Cook the chicken for 2–3 minutes, or until golden brown, then add the sliced celery and mushroom halves and cook for a further 2–3 minutes.

3 Sprinkle in the flour and stir until the chicken and vegetables are coated. Gradually stir the wine into the pan until a thick sauce forms, then stir in the stock and reserved marinade. Bring to the boil, stirring constantly. Cover and simmer for about 10 minutes, then stir in the remaining basil.

4 Meanwhile, bring a large saucepan of lightly salted water to the boil. Slowly add the linguine and simmer for 7–10 minutes, or until 'al dente'. Drain well and turn into a large serving bowl, pour over the sauce and garnish with the lemon zest and fresh basil leaves. Serve immediately.

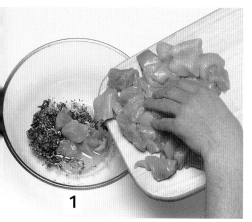

1

2

3

Lemon Chicken with Potatoes, Rosemary & Olives

INGREDIENTS

Serves 6

12 skinless boneless chicken thighs
1 large lemon
125 ml/4 fl oz extra virgin olive oil
6 garlic cloves, peeled and sliced
2 onions, peeled and thinly sliced
bunch of fresh rosemary
1.1 kg/2½ lb potatoes, peeled and cut
  into 4 cm/1½ inch pieces
salt and freshly ground black pepper
18–24 black olives, pitted

To serve:
steamed carrots
courgettes

HELPFUL HINT

It is worth seeking out unwaxed lemons for this recipe, or for any recipe in which the lemon zest is to be eaten. If unwaxed fruit are unavailable, pour hot water over and scrub well before removing the zest.

1 Preheat oven to 200°C/400°F/Gas Mark 6, 15 minutes before cooking. Trim the chicken thighs and place in a shallow baking dish large enough to hold them in a single layer. Remove the rind from the lemon with a zester or, if using a peeler, cut into thin julienne strips. Reserve half and add the remainder to the chicken. Squeeze the lemon juice over the chicken, toss to coat well and leave to stand for 10 minutes.

2 Transfer the chicken to a roasting tin. Add the remaining lemon zest or julienne strips, olive oil, garlic, onions and half of the rosemary sprigs. Toss gently and leave for about 20 minutes.

3 Cover the potatoes with lightly salted water and bring to the boil. Cook for 2 minutes, then drain well and add to the chicken. Season to taste with salt and pepper.

4 Roast the chicken in the preheated oven for 50 minutes, turning frequently and basting, or until the chicken is cooked. Just before the end of cooking time, discard the rosemary, and add fresh sprigs of rosemary. Add the olives and stir. Serve immediately with steamed carrots and courgettes.

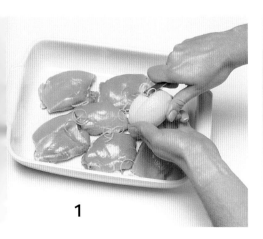

1

2

4

Persian Chicken Pilaf

INGREDIENTS

Serves 4–6

2–3 tbsp vegetable oil

700 g/1½ lb boneless skinless
  chicken pieces (breast and thighs),
  cut into 2.5 cm/1 inch pieces

2 medium onions, peeled and
  coarsely chopped

1 tsp ground cumin

200 g/7 oz long-grain white rice

1 tbsp tomato purée

1 tsp saffron strands

salt and freshly ground black pepper

100 ml/3½ fl oz pomegranate juice

900 ml/1½ pints chicken stock

125 g/4 oz ready-to-eat dried apricots
  or prunes, halved

2 tbsp raisins

2 tbsp freshly chopped mint or parsley

pomegranate seeds,
  to garnish (optional)

1 Heat the oil in a large heavy-based saucepan over a medium-high heat. Cook the chicken pieces, in batches, until lightly browned. Return all the browned chicken to the saucepan.

2 Add the onions to the saucepan, reduce the heat to medium and cook for 3–5 minutes, stirring frequently, until the onions begin to soften. Add the cumin and rice and stir to coat the rice. Cook for about 2 minutes until the rice is golden and translucent. Stir in the tomato purée and the saffron strands, then season to taste with salt and pepper.

3 Add the pomegranate juice and stock and bring to the boil, stirring once or twice. Add the apricots or prunes and raisins and stir gently. Reduce the heat to low and cook for 30 minutes until the chicken and rice are tender and the liquid is absorbed.

4 Turn into a shallow serving dish and sprinkle with the chopped mint or parsley. Serve immediately, garnished with pomegranate seeds, if using.

Steamed, Crispy, Citrus Chicken

INGREDIENTS

Serves 6

200 ml/7 fl oz light soy sauce
1 tbsp brown sugar
4 star anise
2 slices fresh root ginger, peeled
5 spring onions, trimmed and sliced
1 small orange, cut into wedges
1 lime, cut into wedges
1.1 kg/2½ lb chicken
2 garlic cloves, peeled and
  finely chopped
2 tbsp Chinese rice wine
2 tbsp dark soy sauce
300 ml/½ pint groundnut oil
orange slices, to garnish
freshly cooked steamed rice, to serve

TASTY TIP

If you prefer, serve the shredded chicken with ready-made Chinese pancakes which have been spread with a little hoisin sauce. Top with shredded spring onions and cucumber and roll up.

1 Pour the light soy sauce and 200 ml/7 fl oz water into the wok and add the sugar and star anise. Bring to the boil over a gentle heat. Pour into a small bowl and leave to cool slightly. Wipe the wok clean with absorbent kitchen paper.

2 Put the ginger, 2 spring onions, orange and lime inside the cavity of the chicken. Place a rack in the wok and pour in boiling water to a depth of 5 cm/2 inches. Put a piece of tinfoil onto the rack and place the chicken in the centre, then pour over the soy sauce mixture.

3 Cover the wok and steam gently for 1–1 hour 10 minutes, or until the chicken is cooked through, pouring off excess fat from time to time. Add more water if necessary. Leave the chicken to cool and dry for up to 3 hours, then cut the chicken into quarters.

4 Mix together the garlic, Chinese rice wine, dark soy sauce and remaining spring onions, then reserve. Dry the wok and heat again, then add the oil. When hot, shallow fry the chicken quarters for 4 minutes, or until golden and crisp. Do this 1 portion at a time, remove and drain on absorbent kitchen paper.

5 When cool enough to handle, shred into bite-sized pieces and drizzle over the sauce. Garnish with slices of orange and serve with freshly steamed rice.

2

4

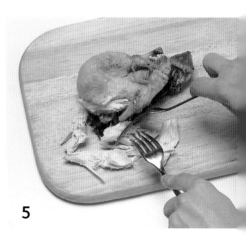

5

Turkey Hash with Potato & Beetroot

INGREDIENTS

Serves 4–6

2 tbsp vegetable oil

50 g/2 oz butter

4 slices streaky bacon, diced or sliced

1 medium onion, peeled and
  finely chopped

450 g/1 lb cooked turkey, diced

450 g/1 lb finely chopped
  cooked potatoes

2–3 tbsp freshly chopped parsley

2 tbsp plain flour

250 g/9 oz cooked medium
  beetroot, diced

green salad, to serve

TASTY TIP

A hash is usually made just with potatoes, but here they are combined with ruby red beetroot, which adds vibrant colour and a sweet earthy flavour to the dish. Make sure that you buy plainly cooked beetroot, rather than the type preserved in vinegar.

1   In a large, heavy-based frying pan, heat the oil and half the butter over a medium heat until sizzling. Add the bacon and cook for 4 minutes, or until crisp and golden, stirring occasionally. Using a slotted spoon, transfer to a large bowl. Add the onion to the pan and cook for 3–4 minutes, or until soft and golden, stirring frequently.

2   Meanwhile, add the turkey, potatoes, parsley and flour to the cooked bacon in the bowl. Stir and toss gently, then fold in the diced beetroot.

3   Add half the remaining butter to the frying pan and then the turkey vegetable mixture. Stir, then spread the mixture to evenly cover the bottom of the frying pan. Cook for 15 minutes, or until the underside is crisp and brown, pressing the hash firmly into a cake with a spatula. Remove from the heat.

4   Invert a large plate over the frying pan and, holding the plate and frying pan together with an oven glove, turn the hash out onto the plate. Heat the remaining butter in the pan, slide the hash back into the pan and cook for 4 minutes, or until crisp and brown on the other side. Invert onto the plate again and serve immediately with a green salad.

2

3

3

Warm Chicken & Potato Salad with Peas & Mint

INGREDIENTS

Serves 4–6

450 g/1 lb new potatoes, peeled
  or scrubbed and cut into
  bite-sized pieces
salt and freshly ground black pepper
2 tbsp cider vinegar
175 g/6 oz frozen garden peas,
  thawed
1 small ripe avocado
4 cooked chicken breasts, about 450
  g/1 lb in weight, skinned and diced
2 tbsp freshly chopped mint
2 heads little gem lettuce
fresh mint sprigs, to garnish

For the dressing:

2 tbsp raspberry or sherry vinegar
2 tsp Dijon mustard
1 tsp clear honey
50 ml/2 fl oz sunflower oil
50 ml/2 fl oz extra virgin olive oil

1 Cook the potatoes in lightly salted boiling water for 15 minutes, or until just tender when pierced with the tip of a sharp knife; do not overcook. Rinse under cold running water to cool slightly, then drain and turn into a large bowl. Sprinkle with the cider vinegar and toss gently.

2 Run the peas under hot water to ensure that they are thawed, pat dry with absorbent kitchen paper and add to the potatoes.

3 Cut the avocado in half lengthways and remove the stone. Peel and cut the avocado into cubes and add to the potatoes and peas. Add the chicken and stir together lightly.

4 To make the dressing, place all the ingredients in a screw-top jar, with a little salt and pepper, and shake well to mix; add a little more oil if the flavour is too sharp. Pour over the salad and toss gently to coat. Sprinkle in half the mint and stir lightly.

5 Separate the lettuce leaves and spread onto a large shallow serving plate. Spoon the salad on top and sprinkle with the remaining mint. Garnish with mint sprigs and serve.

1

3

4

Chicken Parcels with Courgettes & Pasta

INGREDIENTS

Serves 4

2 tbsp olive oil

125 g/4 oz farfalle pasta

1 onion, peeled and thinly sliced

1 garlic clove, peeled and
    finely chopped

2 medium courgettes, trimmed and
    thinly sliced

salt and freshly ground black pepper

2 tbsp freshly chopped oregano

4 plum tomatoes, deseeded and
    coarsely chopped

4 x 175 g/6 oz boneless, skinless
    chicken breasts

150 ml/¼ pint Italian white wine

1 Preheat oven to 200°C/400°F/Gas Mark 6, 15 minutes before cooking. Lightly brush 4 large sheets of non-stick baking parchment with half the oil. Bring a saucepan of lightly salted water to the boil and cook the pasta for 10 minutes, or until 'al dente'. Drain and reserve.

2 Heat the remaining oil in a frying pan and cook the onion for 2–3 minutes. Add the garlic and cook for 1 minute. Add the courgettes and cook for 1 minute, then remove from the heat, season to taste with salt and pepper and add half the oregano.

3 Divide the cooked pasta equally between the 4 sheets of baking parchment, positioning the pasta in the centre. Top the pasta with equal amounts of the vegetable mixture, and sprinkle a quarter of the chopped tomatoes over each.

4 Score the surface of each chicken breast about 1 cm/½ inch deep. Place a chicken breast on top of the pasta and sprinkle each with the remaining oregano and the white wine. Fold the edges of the paper along the top, then along each side, creating a sealed envelope.

5 Bake in the preheated oven for 30–35 minutes, or until cooked. Serve immediately.

HELPFUL HINT

This is a great recipe for entertaining. The parcels can be prepared ahead and baked when needed. For a dramatic presentation, serve in the paper.

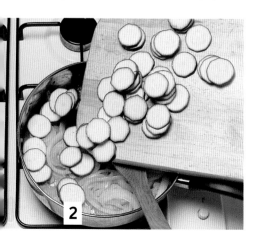

2

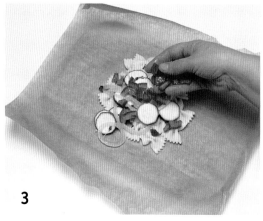

3

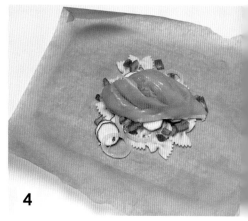

4

Chicken with Roasted Fennel & Citrus Rice

INGREDIENTS

Serves 4

2 tsp fennel seeds
1 tbsp freshly chopped oregano
1 garlic clove, peeled and crushed
salt and freshly ground black pepper
4 chicken quarters, about
  175 g/6 oz each
½ lemon, finely sliced
1 fennel bulb, trimmed
2 tsp olive oil
4 plum tomatoes
25 g/1 oz stoned green olives

To garnish:
fennel fronds, orange slices

For the citrus rice:
225 g/8 oz long-grain rice
finely grated rind and juice of ½ lemon
150 ml/¼ pint orange juice
450 ml/¾ pint boiling chicken or
  vegetable stock

1 Preheat the oven to 200°C/400°F/Gas Mark 6. Lightly crush the fennel seeds and mix with oregano, garlic, salt and pepper. Place between the skin and flesh of the chicken breasts, careful not to tear the skin. Arrange the lemon slices on top of the chicken.

2 Cut the fennel into 8 wedges. Place on baking tray with the chicken. Lightly brush the fennel with the oil. Cook the chicken and fennel on the top shelf of the preheated oven for 10 minutes.

3 Meanwhile, put the rice in a 2.3 litre/4 pint ovenproof dish. Stir in the lemon rind and juice, orange juice and stock. Cover with a lid and put on the middle shelf of the oven.

4 Reduce the oven temperature to 180°C/350°F/Gas Mark 4. Cook the chicken for a further 40 minutes, turning the fennel wedges and lemon slices once. Deseed and chop the tomatoes. Add to the tray and cook for 5–10 minutes. Remove from the oven.

5 When cooled slightly, remove the chicken skin and discard. Fluff the rice, scatter olives over the dish. Garnish with fennel fronds, orange slices and serve.

1

3

4

Spiced Indian Roast Potatoes with Chicken

INGREDIENTS

Serves 4

700 g/1½ lb waxy potatoes, peeled
  and cut into large chunks
salt and freshly ground black pepper
4 tbsp sunflower oil
8 chicken drumsticks
1 large Spanish onion, peeled and
  roughly chopped
3 shallots, peeled and
  roughly chopped
2 large garlic cloves, peeled
  and crushed
1 red chilli
2 tsp fresh root ginger, peeled and
  finely grated
2 tsp ground cumin
2 tsp ground coriander
pinch of cayenne pepper
4 cardamom pods, crushed
sprigs of fresh coriander, to garnish

1 Preheat the oven to 190°C/375°F/Gas Mark 5, about 10 minutes before cooking. Parboil the potatoes for 5 minutes in lightly salted boiling water, then drain thoroughly and reserve. Heat the oil in a large frying pan, add the chicken drumsticks and cook until sealed on all sides. Remove and reserve.

2 Add the onions and shallots to the pan and fry for 4–5 minutes, or until softened. Stir in the garlic, chilli and ginger and cook for 1 minute, stirring constantly. Stir in the ground cumin, coriander, cayenne pepper and crushed cardamom pods and continue to cook, stirring, for a further minute.

3 Add the potatoes to the pan, then add the chicken. Season to taste with salt and pepper. Stir gently until the potatoes and chicken pieces are coated in the onion and spice mixture.

4 Spoon into a large roasting tin and roast in the preheated oven for 35 minutes, or until the chicken and potatoes are cooked thoroughly. Garnish with fresh coriander and serve immediately.

New Orleans Jambalaya

INGREDIENTS

Serves 6–8

For the seasoning mix:

2 dried bay leaves

1 tsp salt

2 tsp cayenne pepper, or to taste

2 tsp dried oregano

1 tsp each ground white and black
   pepper, or to taste

3 tbsp vegetable oil

125 g/4 oz ham

225 g/8 oz smoked pork sausage,
   cut into chunks

2 large onions, peeled and chopped

4 celery stalks, trimmed and chopped

2 green peppers, deseeded
   and chopped

2 garlic cloves, peeled and
   finely chopped

350 g/12 oz raw chicken, diced

400 g can chopped tomatoes

600 ml/1 pint fish stock

400 g/14 oz long-grain white rice

4 spring onions, trimmed and
   coarsely chopped

275 g/10 oz raw prawns, peeled

250 g/9 oz white crab meat

1   Mix all the seasoning ingredients together in a small bowl
    and reserve.

2   Heat 2 tablespoons of the oil in a large flameproof casserole over
    a medium heat. Add the ham and sausage and cook, stirring often,
    for 7–8 minutes until golden. Remove from the pan and reserve.

3   Add the onions, celery and peppers to the casserole and cook for
    about 4 minutes, or until softened, stirring occasionally. Stir in the
    garlic, then using a slotted spoon, transfer all the vegetables to a
    plate and reserve with the sausage.

4   Add the chicken pieces to the casserole and cook for about
    4 minutes, or until beginning to colour, turning once. Stir in the
    seasoning mix and turn the pieces to coat well. Return the sausage
    and vegetables to the casserole and stir well. Add the chopped
    tomatoes, with their juice, and the stock and bring to the boil.

5   Stir in the rice and reduce the heat to low. Cover and simmer for
    12 minutes. Uncover, stir in the spring onions and prawns and cook,
    covered, for a further 4 minutes. Add the crab and gently stir in.
    Cook for 2–3 minutes, or until the rice is tender. Remove from
    the heat, cover and leave to stand for 5 minutes before serving.

2

4

5

Spatchcocked Poussins with Garlic Sage Butter

INGREDIENTS

Serves 4

For the herb butter:
6 large garlic cloves
150 g/5 oz butter, softened
2 tbsp freshly snipped chives
2 tbsp freshly chopped sage
grated rind and juice of 1 lemon
salt and ground black pepper

For the poussins:
4 spatchcocked poussins
2 tbsp extra virgin olive oil

To garnish:
chives
fresh sage leaves

To serve:
grilled quick-cook polenta
grilled tomatoes

1 Preheat grill and line the grill rack with tinfoil, before cooking. Put the garlic cloves in a small saucepan and cover with cold water. Bring to the boil, then simmer for 5 minutes, or until softened. Drain and cool slightly. Cut off the root end of each clove and squeeze the softened garlic into a bowl.

2 Pound the garlic until smooth, then beat in the butter, chives, sage and lemon rind and juice. Season to taste with salt and pepper.

3 Gently loosen the skin from each poussin breast by sliding your hand between the skin and the flesh. Push one-quarter of the herb butter under the skin, spreading evenly over the breast and the top of the thighs. Pull the neck skin gently to tighten the skin over the breast and tuck under the bird. Repeat with the remaining birds and herb butter.

4 Thread two wooden skewers crossways through each bird, from one wing through the opposite leg, to keep the poussin flat. Repeat with the remaining birds, brush with the olive oil and season with salt and pepper.

5 Arrange the poussins on the rack over the foil-lined rack and grill for 25 minutes, turning occasionally, until golden and crisp and the juices run clear when a thigh is pierced with a sharp knife or skewer. (Position the rack about 12.5 cm/5 inches from the heat source or the skin will brown before the birds are cooked through). Garnish with chives and sage leaves and serve immediately with grilled polenta and a few grilled tomatoes.

2

4

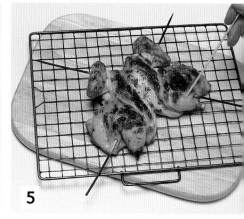

5

Wild Mushroom Risotto

INGREDIENTS

Serves 4

15 g/½ oz dried porcini
1.1 litres/2 pints vegetable stock
75 g/3 oz butter
1 tbsp olive oil
1 onion, peeled and chopped
2–4 garlic cloves, peeled
  and chopped
1–2 red chillies, deseeded
  and chopped
225 g/8 oz wild mushrooms, wiped
  and halved, if large
125 g/4 oz button mushrooms,
  wiped and sliced
350 g/12 oz Arborio rice
175 g/6 oz large cooked
  prawns, peeled
150 ml/¼ pint white wine
salt and freshly ground black pepper
1 tbsp lemon zest
1 tbsp freshly snipped chives
2 tbsp freshly chopped parsley

1 Soak the porcini in 300 ml/½ pint of very hot, but not boiling, water for 30 minutes. Drain, reserving the mushrooms and soaking liquid. Pour the stock into a saucepan, and bring to the boil, then reduce the heat to keep it simmering.

2 Melt the butter and oil in a large deep frying pan, add the onion, garlic and chillies and cook gently for 5 minutes. Add the wild and button mushrooms with the drained porcini, and continue to cook for 4–5 minutes, stirring frequently.

3 Stir in the rice and cook for 1 minute. Strain the reserved soaking liquid and stir into the rice with a little of the hot stock. Cook gently, stirring frequently, until the liquid is absorbed. Continue to add most of the stock, a ladleful at a time, cooking after each addition, until the rice is tender and the risotto looks creamy.

4 Add the prawns and wine along with the last additions of stock. When the prawns are hot and all the liquid is absorbed, season to taste with salt and pepper. Remove from the heat and stir in the lemon zest, chives and parsley, reserving some for the garnish. Garnish and serve.

1

4

4

Duck & Exotic Fruit Stir Fry

INGREDIENTS

Serves 4

4 duck breast fillets, skinned
    removed and cut into strips

½ tsp Chinese five spice powder

2 tbsp soy sauce

1 tbsp sesame oil

1 tbsp groundnut oil

2 celery stalks, trimmed and diced

225 g can pineapples chunks, drained

1 mango, peeled, stoned and cut
    into chunks

125 g/4 oz lychees, peeled if fresh,
    stoned and halved

125 ml/4 fl oz chicken stock

2 tbsp tomato paste

2 tbsp plum sauce

2 tsp wine vinegar

pinch of soft brown sugar

toasted nuts, to garnish

steamed rice, to serve

TASTY TIP

The exotic fruit in this recipe not
only looks beautiful, but helps to
cut through the richness of the
duck meat. Do not overcook the
duck or it will become dry.

1   Place the duck strips in a shallow bowl. Mix together the Chinese
five spice powder, soy sauce and sesame oil, pour over the duck and
marinate for 2 hours in the refrigerator. Stir occasionally during
marinating. Remove the duck from the marinade and reserve.

2   Heat the wok, add the oil and when hot, stir-fry the marinated duck
strips for 4 minutes. Remove from the wok and reserve.

3   Add the celery to the wok and stir-fry for 2 minutes, then add the
pineapple, mango and lychees and stir-fry for a further 3 minutes.
Return the duck to the wok.

4   Mix together the chicken stock, tomato paste, plum sauce, wine
vinegar and a pinch of brown sugar. Add to the wok, bring to the
boil and simmer, stirring, for 2 minutes. Sprinkle with the nuts
and serve immediately with the freshly steamed rice.

1

2

4

Crispy Aromatic Duck

INGREDIENTS

Serves 4

2 tbsp Chinese five spice powder

75 g/3 oz Szechuan peppercorns,
  lightly crushed

25 g/1 oz whole black peppercorns,
  lightly crushed

3 tbsp cumin seeds, lightly crushed

200 g/7 oz rock salt

2.7 kg/6 lb oven-ready duck

7.5 cm/3 inch piece fresh root ginger,
  peeled and cut into 6 slices

6 spring onions, trimmed and cut
  into 7.5 cm/3 inch lengths

cornflour for dusting

1.1 litres/2 pints groundnut oil

To serve:

warm Chinese pancakes

spring onion, cut into shreds

cucumber, cut into slices lengthways

hoisin sauce

TASTY TIP

To serve 4–6 people, you will need
about 20 pancakes. Brush or spray
each with a little water and a few
drops of sesame oil. Layer them in
a steamer on a plate and warm
through for 10 minutes.

1 Mix together the Chinese five spice powder, Szechuan and black peppercorns, cumin seeds and salt. Rub the duck inside and out with the spice mixture. Wrap the duck with clingfilm and place in the refrigerator for 24 hours. Brush any loose spices from the duck. Place the ginger and spring onions into the duck cavity and put the duck on a heatproof plate.

2 Place a wire rack in a wok and pour in boiling water to a depth of 5 cm/2 inches. Lower the duck and plate on to the rack and cover. Steam gently for 2 hours or until the duck is cooked through, pouring off excess fat from time to time and adding more water, if necessary. Remove the duck, pour off all the liquid and discard the ginger and spring onions. Leave the duck in a cool place for 2 hours, or until it has dried and cooled.

3 Cut the duck into quarters and dust lightly with cornflour. Heat the oil in a wok or deep-fat fryer to 190°C/375°F, then deep-fry the duck quarters 2 at a time. Cook the breast for 8–10 minutes and the thighs and legs for 12–14 minutes, or until each piece is heated through. Drain on absorbent kitchen paper, then shred with a fork. Serve immediately with warm Chinese pancakes, spring onion shreds, cucumber slices and hoisin sauce.

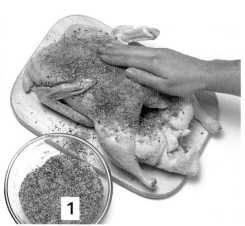

1

2

3

Duck Lasagna with Porcini

INGREDIENTS

Serves 4

1.4–1.8 kg/3–4 lb duck, quartered
1 onion, unpeeled and quartered
2 carrots, peeled and cut into pieces
1 celery stalk, cut into pieces
1 leek, trimmed and cut into pieces
2 garlic cloves, unpeeled
  and smashed
1 tbsp black peppercorns
2 bay leaves
6–8 sprigs of fresh thyme
50 g/2 oz dried porcini mushrooms
125 ml/4 oz dry sherry
75 g/3 oz butter, diced
1 bunch of fresh basil leaves, stripped
  from stems
24 precooked lasagna sheets
75 g/3 oz Parmesan cheese, grated
sprig of parsley

To serve:

mixed salad

1 Preheat oven to 180°C/350°F/Gas Mark 4. Put the duck with the vegetables, garlic, peppercorns, bay leaves and thyme into a large stock pot and cover with cold water. Bring to the boil, skimming off any fat, then reduce the heat and simmer for 1 hour. Transfer the duck to a bowl and cool slightly.

2 When cool, remove the meat from the duck and dice. Return all the bones and trimmings to the simmering stock and continue to simmer for 1 hour. Strain the stock into a large bowl and leave until cold. Remove the fat that has risen to the top of the stock.

3 Put the porcini in a colander and rinse. Leave for 1 minute to dry off, then turn out on to a chopping board and chop finely. Place in a small bowl, then pour over the sherry and leave for about 1 hour.

4 Heat 25 g/1 oz of the butter in a frying pan. Shred the basil leaves and add to the hot butter, stirring until wilted. Add the soaked porcini and any liquid, mix well and reserve.

5 Oil a 30.5 x 23 cm/12 x 9 inch deep baking dish and pour a little stock into the base. Cover with 6–8 lasagna sheets, making sure that sheets slightly overlap. Continue to layer the pasta with a little stock, duck meat, the mushroom-basil mixture and Parmesan. Add a little butter every other layer.

6 Cover with tinfoil and bake in the preheated oven for 40–45 minutes, Stand for 10 minutes before serving. Garnish with a sprig of parsley and serve with salad.

1

2

3

Hot-&-Sour Duck

INGREDIENTS

Serves 4

4 small boneless duck breasts, with
   skin on, thinly sliced on the diagonal
1 tsp salt
4 tbsp tamarind pulp
4 shallots, peeled and chopped
2 garlic cloves, peeled and chopped
2.5 cm/1 inch piece fresh root
   ginger, chopped
1 tsp ground coriander
3 large red chillies, deseeded
   and chopped
½ tsp turmeric
6 blanched almonds, chopped
125 ml/4 fl oz vegetable oil
227 g can bamboo shoots, drained,
   rinsed and finely sliced
salt and freshly ground black pepper
sprigs of fresh coriander, to garnish
freshly cooked rice, to serve

FOOD FACT

Although bamboo shoots are virtually flavourless, they add a fresh flavour and crunchiness to dishes. Occasionally they can be bought fresh, but the canned version is inexpensive and almost as good.

1. Sprinkle the duck with the salt, cover lightly and refrigerate for 20 minutes.

2. Meanwhile, place the tamarind pulp in a small bowl, pour over 4 tablespoons of hot water and leave for 2–3 minutes or until softened. Press the mixture through a sieve into another bowl to produce about 2 tablespoons of smooth juice.

3. Place the tamarind juice in a food processor with the shallots, garlic, ginger, coriander, chillies, turmeric and almonds. Blend until smooth, adding a little more hot water if necessary, and reserve the paste.

4. Heat a wok or large frying pan, add the oil and when hot, stir-fry the duck in batches for about 3 minutes, or until just coloured, then drain on absorbent kitchen paper.

5. Discard all but 2 tablespoons of the oil in the wok. Return to the heat. Add the paste and stir-fry for 5 minutes. Add the duck and stir-fry for 2 minutes. Add the bamboo shoots and stir-fry for 2 minutes. Season to taste with salt and pepper. Turn into a warmed serving dish, garnish with a sprig of fresh coriander and serve immediately with rice.

1

3

5

Teriyaki Duck with Plum Chutney

INGREDIENTS

Serves 4

4 tbsp Japanese soy sauce

4 tbsp dry sherry

2 garlic cloves, peeled and
   finely chopped

2.5 cm/1 inch piece fresh root ginger,
   peeled and finely chopped

350 g/12 oz skinless duck breast
   fillets, cut in chunks

2 tbsp groundnut oil

225 g/8 oz carrots, peeled and cut
   into fine strips

½ cucumber, cut into strips

5 spring onions, trimmed
   and shredded

toasted almonds, to garnish

freshly cooked egg noodles,
   to serve

For the plum chutney:

25 g/1 oz butter

1 red onion, peeled and
   finely chopped

2 tsp soft brown sugar

4 plums, stoned and halved

zest and juice of ½ orange

50 g/2 oz raisins

1 Mix together the soy sauce, sherry, garlic and ginger and pour into a shallow dish. Add the duck strips and stir until coated in the marinade. Cover and leave in the refrigerator for 30 minutes.

2 Meanwhile make the plum chutney. Melt the butter in a wok, add the onion and sugar and cook gently over a low heat for 20 minutes. Add the plums, orange zest and juice and simmer for 10 minutes, then stir in the raisins. Spoon into a small bowl and wipe the wok clean. Drain the duck, reserving the marinade.

3 Heat the wok, add the oil and when hot, add the carrots, cucumber and spring onions. Stir-fry for 2 minutes, or until tender. Remove and reserve.

4 Add the drained duck to the wok and stir-fry over a high heat for 2 minutes. Return the vegetables to the wok and add the reserved marinade. Stir-fry briefly, until heated through.

5 Garnish the duck with the toasted almonds and serve immediately with freshly cooked noodles and the plum chutney.

1

2

3

Turkey & Vegetable Stir Fry

INGREDIENTS

Serves 4

350 g/12 oz mixed vegetables, such
    as baby sweetcorn, 1 small red
    pepper, pak choi, mushrooms,
    broccoli florets and baby carrots
1 red chilli
2 tbsp groundnut oil
350 g/12 oz skinless, boneless turkey
    breast, sliced into fine strips across
    the grain
2 garlic cloves, peeled and
    finely chopped
2.5 cm/1 inch piece fresh root ginger,
    peeled and finely grated
3 spring onions, trimmed and
    finely sliced
2 tbsp light soy sauce
1 tbsp Chinese rice wine or dry sherry
2 tbsp chicken stock or water
1 tsp cornflour
1 tsp sesame oil
freshly cooked noodles or rice, to serve

To garnish:

50 g/2 oz toasted cashew nuts
2 spring onions, finely shredded
25 g/1 oz beansprouts

1   Slice or chop the vegetables into small pieces, depending on which you use. Halve the baby sweetcorn lengthways, deseed and thinly slice the red pepper, tear or shred the pak choi, slice the mushrooms, break the broccoli into small florets and cut the carrots into matchsticks. Deseed and finely chop the chilli.

2   Heat a wok or large frying pan, add the oil and when hot, add the turkey strips and stir-fry for 1 minute or until they turn white. Add the garlic, ginger, spring onions and chilli and cook for a few seconds.

3   Add the prepared carrot, pepper, broccoli and mushrooms and stir-fry for 1 minute. Add the baby sweetcorn and pak choi and stir-fry for 1 minute.

4   Blend the soy sauce, Chinese rice wine or sherry and stock or water and pour over the vegetables. Blend the cornflour with 1 teaspoon of water and stir into the vegetables, mixing well. Bring to the boil, reduce the heat, then simmer for 1 minute. Stir in the sesame oil. Tip into a warmed serving dish, sprinkle with cashew nuts, shredded spring onions and beansprouts. Serve immediately with noodles or rice.

Stir–Fried Duck with Cashews

INGREDIENTS

Serves 4

450 g/1 lb duck breast, skinned

3 tbsp groundnut oil

1 garlic clove, peeled and
  finely chopped

1 tsp freshly grated ginger root

1 carrot, peeled and sliced

125 g/4 oz mangetout, trimmed

2 tsp Chinese rice wine or dry sherry

1 tbsp light soy sauce

1 tsp cornflour

50 g/2 oz unsalted cashew
  nuts, roasted

1 spring onion, trimmed and
  finely chopped

1 spring onion, shredded

boiled or steamed rice, to serve

HELPFUL HINT

Look for small, flat, bright green mangetout containing, barely formed peas. Store in the refrigerator for no more than 2 days before using. To prepare, top and tail, pulling away as much string from the edges as you can. Dry-fry the cashew nuts in the wok before starting to seal the duck breasts. Ensure they do not burn.

1 Trim the duck breasts, discarding any fat and slice thickly. Heat the wok, add 2 tablespoons of the oil and when hot, add the sliced duck breast. Cook for 3–4 minutes or until sealed. Using a slotted spoon, remove from the wok and leave to drain on absorbent kitchen paper.

2 Wipe the wok clean and return to the heat. Add the remaining oil and when hot, add the garlic and ginger. Stir-fry for 30 seconds, then add the carrot and mangetout. Stir-fry for a further 2 minutes, then pour in the Chinese rice wine or sherry and soy sauce.

3 Blend the cornflour with 1 teaspoon of water and stir into the wok. Mix well and bring to the boil. Return the duck slices to the wok and simmer for 5 minutes, or until the meat and vegetables are tender. Add the cashews, then remove the wok from the heat.

4 Sprinkle over the chopped and shredded spring onion and serve immediately with plain boiled or steamed rice.

1

2

3

Turkey Tetrazzini

INGREDIENTS

Serves 4

275 g/10 oz green and
  white tagliatelle
50 g/2 oz butter
4 slices streaky bacon, diced
1 onion, peeled and finely chopped
175 g/6 oz mushrooms, thinly sliced
40 g/1½ oz plain flour
450 ml/¾ pint chicken stock
150 ml/¼ pint double cream
2 tbsp sherry
450 g/1 lb cooked turkey meat, cut
  into bite-sized pieces
1 tbsp freshly chopped parsley
freshly grated nutmeg
salt and freshly ground black pepper
25 g/1 oz Parmesan cheese, grated

To garnish:
freshly chopped parsley
Parmesan cheese, grated

1 Preheat oven to 180°C/350°F/Gas Mark 4. Lightly oil a large ovenproof dish. Bring a large saucepan of lightly salted water to the boil. Add the tagliatelle and cook for 7–9 minutes, or until 'al dente'. Drain well and reserve.

2 In a heavy-based saucepan, heat the butter and add the bacon. Cook for 2–3 minutes, or until crisp and golden. Add the onion and mushrooms and cook for 3–4 minutes, or until the vegetables are tender.

3 Stir in the flour and cook for 2 minutes. Remove from the heat and slowly stir in the stock. Return to the heat and cook, stirring until a smooth, thick sauce has formed. Add the tagliatelle, then pour in the cream and sherry. Add the turkey and parsley. Season to taste with the nutmeg and salt and pepper. Toss well to coat.

4 Turn the mixture into the prepared dish, spreading evenly. Sprinkle the top with the Parmesan cheese and bake in the preheated oven for 30–35 minutes, or until crisp, golden and bubbling. Garnish with chopped parsley and Parmesan cheese. Serve straight from the dish.

TASTY TIP
This is a great way to use Christmas leftovers – it is worth putting extra meat in the freezer. Use frozen leftovers within 1 month.

1

2

3

Aromatic Duck Burgers on Potato Pancakes

INGREDIENTS

Serves 4

700 g/1½ lb boneless duck breasts

2 tbsp hoisin sauce

1 garlic clove, peeled and finely chopped

4 spring onions, trimmed and finely chopped

2 tbsp Japanese soy sauce

½ tsp Chinese five spice powder

salt and freshly ground black pepper

freshly chopped coriander, to garnish

extra hoisin sauce, to serve

For the potato pancakes:

450 g/1 lb floury potatoes

1 small onion, peeled and grated

1 small egg, beaten

1 heaped tbsp plain flour

1 Peel off the thick layer of fat from the duck breasts and cut into small pieces. Put the fat in a small dry saucepan and set over a low heat for 10–15 minutes, or until the fat runs clear and the crackling goes crisp; reserve.

2 Cut the duck meat into pieces and blend in a food processor until coarsely chopped. Spoon into a bowl and add the hoisin sauce, garlic, half the spring onions, soy sauce and Chinese five spice powder. Season to taste with salt and pepper and shape into 4 burgers. Cover and chill in the refrigerator for 1 hour.

3 To make the potato pancakes, grate the potatoes into a large bowl, squeeze out the water with your hands, then put on a clean tea towel and twist the ends to squeeze out any remaining water. Return the potato to the bowl, add the onion and egg and mix well. Add the flour and salt and pepper. Stir to blend.

4 Heat about 2 tablespoons of the clear duck fat in a large frying pan. Spoon the potato mixture into 2–4 pattie shapes and cook for 6 minutes, or until golden and crisp, turning once. Keep warm in the oven. Repeat with the remaining mixture, adding duck fat as needed.

5 Preheat the grill and line the grill rack with tinfoil. Brush the burgers with a little of the duck fat and grill for 6–8 minutes, or longer if wished, turning once. Arrange 1–2 potato pancakes on a plate and top with a burger. Spoon over a little hoisin sauce and garnish with the remaining spring onions and coriander.

1

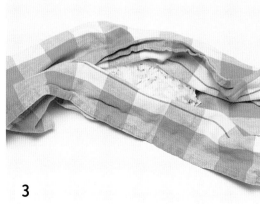

3

= 4

Chicken Satay Salad

INGREDIENTS

Serves 4

4 tbsp crunchy peanut butter
1 tbsp chilli sauce
1 garlic clove, peeled and crushed
2 tbsp cider vinegar
2 tbsp light soy sauce
2 tbsp dark soy sauce
2 tsp soft brown sugar
pinch of salt
2 tsp freshly ground
   Szechuan peppercorns
450 g/1 lb dried egg noodles
2 tbsp sesame oil
1 tbsp groundnut oil
450 g/1 lb skinless, boneless chicken
   breast fillets, cut into cubes
shredded celery leaves, to garnish
cos lettuce, to serve

FOOD FACT

Szechuan peppercorns are the dried berries of a shrub, which is a member of the citrus family. The smell is reminiscent of lavender and they have a sharp, mildly spicy flavour. They are often toasted in a dry frying pan before grinding, to bring out their distinctive flavour.

1 Place the peanut butter, chilli sauce, garlic, cider vinegar, soy sauces, sugar, salt and ground peppercorns in a food processor and blend to form a smooth paste. Scrape into a bowl, cover and chill in the refrigerator until required.

2 Bring a large saucepan of lightly salted water to the boil. Add the noodles and cook for 3–5 minutes. Drain and plunge into cold water. Drain again and toss in the sesame oil. Leave to cool.

3 Heat the wok until very hot, add the oil and when hot, add the chicken cubes. Stir-fry for 5–6 minutes until the chicken is golden brown and cooked through.

4 Remove the chicken from the wok using a slotted spoon and add to the noodles, together with the peanut sauce. Mix lightly together, then sprinkle with the shredded celery leaves and either serve immediately or leave until cold, then serve with cos lettuce.

1

2

3

Chicken Tikka Masala

INGREDIENTS

Serves 4

4 skinless chicken breast fillets
150 ml/¼ pint natural yogurt
1 garlic clove, peeled and crushed
2.5 cm/1 inch piece fresh root ginger,
   peeled and grated
1 tsp chilli powder
1 tbsp ground coriander
2 tbsp lime juice
twist of lime, to garnish
freshly cooked rice, to serve

For the masala sauce:

15 g/½ oz unsalted butter
2 tbsp sunflower oil
1 onion, peeled and chopped
1 green chilli, deseeded and
   finely chopped
1 tsp garam masala
150 ml/¼ pint double cream
salt and freshly ground black pepper
3 tbsp fresh coriander leaves,
   roughly torn

1   Preheat the oven to 200°C/400°F/Gas Mark 6, 15 minutes before cooking. Cut each chicken breast across into 3 pieces, then make 2 or 3 shallow cuts in each piece. Put in a shallow dish. Mix together the yogurt, garlic, ginger, chilli powder, ground coriander and lime juice. Pour over the chicken, cover and marinate in the refrigerator for up to 24 hours.

2   Remove the chicken from the marinade and arrange on an oiled baking tray. Bake in the preheated oven for 15 minutes, or until golden brown and cooked.

3   While the chicken is cooking, heat the butter and oil in a wok and stir-fry the onion for 5 minutes, or until tender. Add the chilli and garam masala and stir-fry for a few more seconds. Stir in the cream and remaining marinade. Simmer over a low heat for 1 minute, stirring all the time.

4   Add the chicken pieces and cook for a further 1 minute, stirring to coat in the sauce. Season to taste with salt and pepper. Transfer the chicken pieces to a warmed serving plate. Stir the chopped coriander into the sauce, then spoon over the chicken, garnish and serve immediately with freshly cooked rice.

1

3

4

Pan–Cooked Chicken with Thai Spices

INGREDIENTS

Serves 4

4 kaffir lime leaves
5 cm/2 inch piece of root ginger, peeled and chopped
300 ml/½ pint chicken stock, boiling
4 x 175 g/6 oz chicken breasts
2 tsp groundnut oil
5 tbsp coconut milk
1 tbsp fish sauce
2 red chillies, deseeded and finely chopped
225 g/8 oz Thai jasmine rice
1 tbsp lime juice
3 tbsp freshly chopped coriander
salt and freshly ground black pepper

To garnish:
wedges of lime
freshly chopped coriander

FOOD FACT

Fresh kaffir lime leaves can be found in Oriental food stores. Most supermarkets now stock dried kaffir lime leaves. If using dried, crumble lightly and use as above.

1　Lightly bruise the kaffir lime leaves and put in a bowl with the chopped ginger. Pour over the chicken stock, cover and leave to infuse for 30 minutes.

2　Meanwhile, cut each chicken breast into two pieces. Heat the oil in a large, non-stick frying pan or flameproof casserole and brown the chicken pieces for 2–3 minutes on each side.

3　Strain the infused chicken stock into the pan. Half cover the pan with a lid and gently simmer for 10 minutes.

4　Stir in the coconut milk, fish sauce and chopped chillies. Simmer, uncovered for 5–6 minutes, or until the chicken is tender and cooked through and the sauce has reduced slightly.

5　Meanwhile, cook the rice in boiling salted water according to the packet instructions. Drain the rice thoroughly.

6　Stir the lime juice and chopped coriander into the sauce. Season to taste with salt and pepper. Serve the chicken and sauce on a bed of rice. Garnish with wedges of lime and freshly chopped coriander and serve immediately.

1

2

4

Chinese Braised White Chicken with Three Sauces

INGREDIENTS

Serves 4

1.4 kg/3 lb oven-ready chicken

salt

6 spring onions, trimmed

5 cm/2 inch piece fresh root ginger, peeled and sliced

2 tsp Szechuan peppercorns, crushed

2½ tsp sea salt flakes or crushed coarse sea salt

2 tsp freshly grated root ginger

4 tbsp dark soy sauce

4 tbsp sunflower oil

1 tsp caster sugar

2 garlic cloves, finely chopped

3 tbsp light soy sauce

1 tbsp Chinese rice wine or dry sherry

1 tsp sesame oil

3 tbsp rice vinegar

1 small hot red chilli, deseeded and finely sliced

spring onion curls, to garnish

freshly steamed saffron-flavoured rice, to serve

1 Remove any fat from inside the chicken, rub inside and out with ½ teaspoon of salt and leave for 20 minutes. Place 3.4 litres/6 pints water with 2 spring onions and the ginger in a saucepan and bring to the boil. Add the chicken, breast-side down, return to the boil, cover and simmer for 20 minutes. Remove from the heat and leave for 1 hour. Remove the chicken and leave to cool.

2 Dry-fry the Szechuan peppercorns in a non-stick frying pan until they darken slightly and smell aromatic. Crush, mix with the sea salt and reserve.

3 Squeeze the juice from half of the grated ginger, mix with the dark soy sauce, 1 tablespoon of the sunflower oil and half the sugar. Reserve.

4 Finely chop the remaining spring onions and mix with the remaining ginger and garlic in a bowl. Heat the remaining oil to smoking and pour over the onion and ginger. When they stop sizzling, stir in the light soy sauce, Chinese rice wine or sherry and sesame oil. Reserve.

5 Mix together the rice vinegar, remaining sugar and chilli. Stir until the sugar dissolves. Reserve.

6 Remove the skin from the chicken, then remove the legs and cut them in two at the joint. Lift the breast meat away from the carcass in two pieces and slice thickly crossways. Sprinkle the pepper and salt mixture over the chicken, garnish with spring onion curls and serve with the dipping sauces, spring onion mixture and rice.

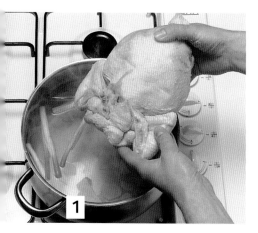

1

2

4

Chinese–Glazed Poussin with Green & Black Rice

INGREDIENTS

Serves 4

4 oven-ready poussins
salt and freshly ground black pepper
300 ml/½ pint apple juice
1 cinnamon stick
2 star anise
½ tsp Chinese five spice powder
50 g/2 oz dark muscovado sugar
2 tbsp tomato ketchup
1 tbsp cider vinegar
grated rind of 1 orange
350 g/12 oz mixed basmati white
   and wild rice
125 g/4 oz mangetout, finely
   sliced lengthways
1 bunch spring onions, trimmed and
   finely shredded lengthways
salt and freshly ground black pepper

1 Preheat the oven to 200°C/400°F/Gas Mark 6, 15 minutes before cooking. Rinse the poussins inside and out and pat dry with absorbent kitchen paper. Using tweezers, remove any feathers. Season well with salt and pepper, then reserve.

2 Pour the apple juice into a small saucepan and add the cinnamon stick, star anise and Chinese five spice powder. Bring to the boil, then simmer rapidly until reduced by half. Reduce the heat, stir in the sugar, tomato ketchup, vinegar and orange rind and simmer gently until the sugar is dissolved and the glaze is syrupy. Remove from the heat and leave to cool completely. Remove the whole spices.

3 Place the poussins on a wire rack set over a tinfoil-lined roasting tin. Brush generously with the apple glaze. Roast in the preheated oven for 40–45 minutes, or until the juices run clear when the thigh is pierced with a skewer, basting once or twice with the remaining glaze. Remove the poussins from the oven and leave to cool slightly.

4 Meanwhile, cook the rice according to the packet instructions. Bring a large saucepan of lightly salted water to the boil and add the mangetout. Blanch for 1 minute, then drain thoroughly. As soon as the rice is cooked, drain and transfer to a warmed bowl. Add the mangetout and spring onions, season to taste and stir well. Arrange on warmed dinner plates, place a poussin on top and serve immediately.

2

3

4

Crispy Chicken Noodles

INGREDIENTS

Serves 4

1 medium egg white
2 tsp cornflour
salt and freshly ground white pepper
225 g/8 oz boneless and skinless
  chicken breast, diced
225 g/8 oz medium Chinese egg
  noodles
200 ml/7 fl oz groundnut oil
2 tbsp Chinese rice wine
2 tbsp oyster sauce
1 tbsp light soy sauce
300 ml/½ pint chicken stock
1 tbsp cornflour

To garnish:
spring onion curls
toasted cashew nuts

1 Mix the egg white with the cornflour in a bowl, season to taste with salt and pepper, then add the chicken and stir to coat. Chill in the refrigerator for 20 minutes. Blanch the noodles for 2 minutes in a large saucepan of boiling salted water and drain.

2 Heat a wok or large frying pan and add 2 tablespoons of the groundnut oil. When hot, spread the noodles evenly over the surface, reduce the heat to low and cook for about 5 minutes, or until browned on one side. Gently turn over, adding extra oil if necessary, and cook until both sides are browned. Reserve and keep warm.

3 Drain the chicken. Wipe the wok clean, reheat and add the remaining groundnut oil. When hot, add the chicken and stir-fry for 2 minutes. Using a slotted spoon, remove and drain on absorbent kitchen paper. Keep warm.

4 Wipe the wok clean, reheat and pour in the Chinese rice wine, oyster sauce, soy sauce and chicken stock and season lightly. Bring to the boil. Blend the cornflour to a paste with 2 tablespoons of water and stir into the wok. Cook, stirring, until the sauce has thickened. Cook for a further 1 minute.

5 Tip the noodles on to warmed plates, top with the crispy chicken pieces and drizzle over the sauce. Garnish with spring onion curls and sprinkle with toasted cashew nuts. Serve immediately.

TASTY TIP
Tossing chicken in a mixture of egg white and cornflour gives it a protective, thin, crispy coating that keeps it succulent.

1

2

4

Rice & Papaya Salad

INGREDIENTS

Serves 4

175 g/6 oz easy-cook basmati rice
1 cinnamon stick, bruised
1 bird's eye chilli, deseeded and
  finely chopped
rind and juice of 2 limes
rind and juice of 2 lemons
2 tbsp Thai fish sauce
1 tbsp soft light brown sugar
1 papaya, peeled and seeds removed
1 mango, peeled and stone removed
1 green chilli, deseeded and
  finely chopped
2 tbsp freshly chopped coriander
1 tbsp freshly chopped mint
250 g/9 oz cooked chicken
50 g/2 oz roasted peanuts, chopped
strips of pitta bread, to serve

1 Rinse and drain the rice and pour into a saucepan. Add 450 ml/
¾ pint boiling salted water and the cinnamon stick. Bring to the boil,
reduce the heat to a very low heat, cover and cook without stirring
for 15–18 minutes, or until all the liquid is absorbed. The rice should
be light and fluffy and have steam holes on the surface. Remove the
cinnamon stick and stir in the rind from 1 lime.

2 To make the dressing, place the bird's eye chilli, remaining rind and
lime and lemon juice, fish sauce and sugar in a food processor, mix
for a few minutes until blended. Alternatively, place all these
ingredients in a screw-top jar and shake until well blended. Pour half
the dressing over the hot rice and toss until the rice glistens.

3 Slice the papaya and mango into thin slices, then place in a bowl.
Add the chopped green chilli, coriander and mint. Place the cooked
chicken on a chopping board, then remove and discard any skin
or sinews. Cut into fine shreds and add to the bowl with the
chopped peanuts.

4 Add the remaining dressing to the chicken mixture and stir until all
the ingredients are lightly coated. Spoon the rice onto a platter, pile
the chicken mixture on top and serve with warm strips of pitta bread.

HELPFUL HINT

The papaya or pawpaw's skin
turns from green when unripe,
through to yellow and orange. To
prepare, cut in half lengthways,
scoop out the black seeds with a
teaspoon and discard. Cut away
the thin skin before slicing.

2

3

3

Singapore Noodles

INGREDIENTS

Serves 4

225 g/8 oz flat rice noodles

3 tbsp sunflower oil

2 shallots, peeled and sliced

2 garlic cloves, peeled and crushed

2 tbsp freshly grated root ginger

1 red pepper, deseeded and
   finely sliced

1 hot red chilli, deseeded and
   finely chopped

175 g/6 oz peeled raw prawns

125 g/4 oz boneless pork, diced

175 g/6 oz boneless chicken, diced

1 tbsp curry powder

1 tsp each crushed fennel seeds and
   ground cinnamon

50 g/2 oz frozen peas, thawed

juice of 1 lemon

3 tbsp fresh coriander leaves

HELPFUL HINT

Use whatever meat or fish you prefer according to taste. This is also a great dish for using up leftover meat, perhaps from the Sunday roast. If using cooked meat, reduce the cooking time accordingly, but make sure that it is piping hot.

1 Put the noodles into a large bowl and pour over boiling water to cover. Leave to stand for 3 minutes, or until slightly underdone according to the packet directions. Drain well and reserve.

2 Heat a wok until almost smoking. Add the oil and carefully swirl around to coat the sides of the wok. Add the shallots, garlic and ginger and cook for a few seconds. Add the pepper and chilli and stir-fry for 3–4 minutes, or until the pepper has softened.

3 Add the prawns, pork, chicken and curry powder to the wok. Stir-fry for a further 4–5 minutes until the meat and prawns are coloured on all sides. Then add the fennel seeds and the ground cinnamon and stir to mix.

4 Add the drained noodles to the wok along with the peas and cook for a further 1–2 minutes until heated through. Add the lemon juice to taste. Sprinkle with the fresh coriander leaves and serve immediately.

2

3

4

Orange Roasted Whole Chicken

INGREDIENTS

Serves 6

1 small orange, thinly sliced

50 g/2 oz sugar

1.4 kg/3 lb oven-ready chicken

1 small bunch fresh coriander

1 small bunch fresh mint

2 tbsp olive oil

1 tsp Chinese five spice powder

½ tsp paprika

1 tsp fennel seeds, crushed

salt and freshly ground black pepper

sprigs of fresh coriander,
   to garnish

freshly cooked vegetables,
   to serve

TASTY TIP

To make oven-baked rice, soften a chopped onion in 1 tablespoon sunflower oil in an ovenproof casserole. Stir in 250 g/9 oz long-grain rice, then remove from the heat. Pour in 750 ml/1¼ pints chicken or vegetable stock, 1 star anise, ½ cinnamon stick, 1 bay leaf, salt and pepper. Cover and cook for 45 minutes or until tender. Fluff up with a fork and remove the spices.

1 Preheat the oven to 190°C/375°F/Gas Mark 5, 10 minutes before cooking. Place the orange slices in a small saucepan, cover with water, bring to the boil, then simmer for 2 minutes and drain. Place the sugar in a clean saucepan with 150 ml/¼ pint fresh water. Stir over a low heat until the sugar dissolves, then bring to the boil, add the drained orange slices and simmer for 10 minutes. Remove from the heat and leave in the syrup until cold.

2 Remove any excess fat from inside the chicken. Starting at the neck end, carefully loosen the skin of the chicken over the breast and legs without tearing. Push the orange slices under the loosened skin with the coriander and mint.

3 Mix together the olive oil, Chinese five spice powder, paprika and crushed fennel seeds and season to taste with salt and pepper. Brush the chicken skin generously with this mixture. Transfer to a wire rack set over a roasting tin and roast in the preheated oven for 1½ hours, or until the juices run clear when a skewer is inserted into the thickest part of the thigh. Remove from the oven and leave to rest for 10 minutes. Garnish with sprigs of fresh coriander and serve with freshly cooked vegetables.

1

2

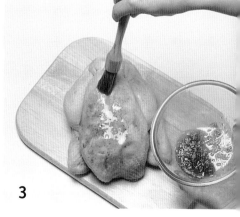

3

Szechuan Sesame Chicken

INGREDIENTS

Serves 4

1 medium egg white
pinch of salt
2 tsp cornflour
450 g/1 lb boneless, skinless chicken
  breast, cut into 7.5 cm/3 inch strips
300 ml/½ pint groundnut oil
1 tbsp sesame seeds
2 tsp dark soy sauce
2 tsp cider vinegar
2 tsp chilli bean sauce
2 tsp sesame oil
2 tsp sugar
1 tbsp Chinese rice wine
1 tsp whole Szechuan
  peppercorns, roasted
2 tbsp spring onion, trimmed and
  finely chopped
mixed salad, to serve

FOOD FACT

Szechuan pepper, also known as anise pepper, is actually the dried red berries of a type of ash tree. Hot and peppery, it should always be roasted before use. To roast, place the 'peppercorns' on a baking tray in a preheated oven at 180°C/ 350°F/Gas Mark 4 for 15 minutes.

1 Beat the egg white with a pinch of salt and the cornflour, pour into a shallow dish and add the chicken strips. Turn to coat, cover with clingfilm and leave in the refrigerator for 20 minutes.

2 Heat a wok, add the groundnut oil and when hot, add the chicken pieces and stir-fry for 2 minutes or until the chicken turns white. Using a slotted spoon, remove the chicken and drain on absorbent kitchen paper. Pour off the oil and reserve 1 tablespoon of the oil. Wipe the wok clean.

3 Reheat the wok, add 1 tablespoon of the groundnut oil with the sesame seeds and stir-fry for 30 seconds, or until golden. Stir in the dark soy sauce, cider vinegar, chilli bean sauce, sesame oil, sugar, Chinese rice wine, Szechuan peppercorns and the spring onions. Bring to the boil.

4 Return the chicken to the wok and stir-fry for 2 minutes, making sure that the chicken is coated evenly with the sauce and sesame seeds. Turn into a warmed serving dish and serve immediately with a mixed salad.

2

3

4

Wild Rice & Bacon Salad with Smoked Chicken

INGREDIENTS

Serves 4

150 g/5 oz wild rice

50 g/2 oz pecan or walnut halves

1 tbsp vegetable oil

4 slices smoked bacon, diced

3–4 shallots, peeled and
  finely chopped

75 ml/3 fl oz walnut oil

2–3 tbsp sherry or cider vinegar

2 tbsp freshly chopped dill

salt and freshly ground black pepper

275 g/10 oz smoked chicken or duck
  breast, thinly sliced

dill sprigs, to garnish

FOOD FACT

Both smoked chicken and duck have a delicate smoky flavour which comes from being first cold-smoked, then briefly hot-smoked. You can, of course, use plain roasted chicken or duck if you prefer.

1 Put the wild rice in a medium saucepan with 600 ml/1 pint water and bring to the boil, stirring once or twice. Reduce the heat, cover and simmer gently for 30–50 minutes, depending on the texture you prefer, chewy or tender. Using a fork, gently fluff into a large bowl and leave to cool slightly.

2 Meanwhile, toast the nuts in a frying pan over a medium heat for 2 minutes, or until they are fragrant and lightly coloured, stirring and tossing frequently. Cool, then chop coarsely and add to the rice.

3 Heat the oil in the frying pan over a medium heat. Add the bacon and cook, stirring from time to time, for 3–4 minutes, or until crisp and brown. Remove from the pan and drain on absorbent kitchen paper. Add the shallots to the pan and cook for 4 minutes, or until just softened, stirring from time to time. Stir into the rice and nuts, with the drained bacon pieces.

4 Whisk the walnut oil, vinegar, half the dill and salt and pepper in a small bowl until combined. Pour the dressing over the rice mixture and toss well to combine. Mix the chicken and the remaining chopped dill into the rice, then spoon into bowls and garnish each serving with a dill sprig. Serve slightly warm, or at room temperature.

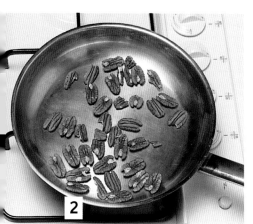

Chinese Barbecue–Style Quails with Aubergines

INGREDIENTS

Serves 6

4 quails
2 tbsp salt
3 tbsp hoisin sauce
1 tbsp Chinese rice wine or dry sherry
1 tbsp light soy sauce
700 g/1½ lb aubergines, trimmed and cubed
1 tbsp oil
4 garlic cloves, peeled and finely chopped
1 tbsp freshly chopped root ginger
6 spring onions, trimmed and finely chopped
3 tbsp dark soy sauce
¼ tsp dried chilli flakes
1 tbsp yellow bean sauce
1 tbsp sugar

To garnish:

sprigs of fresh coriander
sliced red chilli

1 Preheat the oven to 240°C/475°F/Gas Mark 9. Rub the quails inside and out with 1 tablespoon of the salt. Mix together the hoisin sauce, Chinese rice wine or sherry and light soy sauce. Rub the quails inside and out with the sauce. Transfer to a small roasting tin and roast in the preheated oven for 5 minutes. Reduce the heat to 180°C/350°F/Gas Mark 4 and continue to roast for 20 minutes. Turn the oven off and leave the quails for 5 minutes, then remove and leave to rest for 10 minutes.

2 Place the aubergine in a colander and sprinkle with the remaining salt. Leave to drain for 20 minutes, then rinse under cold running water and pat dry with absorbent kitchen paper.

3 Heat a wok or large frying pan over a moderate heat. Add the oil and when hot, add the aubergines, garlic, ginger and 4 of the spring onions and cook for 1 minute. Add the dark soy sauce, chilli flakes, yellow bean sauce, sugar and 450 ml/¾ pint of water. Bring to the boil, then simmer uncovered for 10–15 minutes.

4 Increase the heat to high and continue to cook, stirring occasionally, until the sauce is reduced and slightly thickened. Spoon the aubergine mixture on to warmed individual plates and top with a quail. Garnish with the remaining spring onion, fresh chilli and a sprig of coriander and serve immediately.

1

2

3

Crispy Roast Duck Legs with Pancakes

INGREDIENTS

Serves 6

900 g/2 lb plums, halved

25 g/1 oz butter

2 star anise

1 tsp freshly grated root ginger

50 g/2 oz soft brown sugar

zest and juice of 1 orange

salt and freshly ground black pepper

4 duck legs

3 tbsp dark soy sauce

2 tbsp dark brown sugar

½ cucumber, cut into matchsticks

1 small bunch spring onions,
  trimmed and shredded

18 ready-made Chinese
  pancakes, warmed

1 Preheat the oven to 220°C/425°F/Gas Mark 7, 15 minutes before cooking. Discard stones from plums and place in a saucepan with the butter, star anise, ginger, brown sugar and orange zest and juice. Season to taste with pepper. Cook over a gentle heat until the sugar has dissolved. Bring to the boil, then reduce heat and simmer for 15 minutes, stirring occasionally until the plums are soft and the mixture is thick. Remove the star anise. Leave to cool.

2 Using a fork, prick the duck legs all over. Place in a large bowl and pour boiling water over to remove some of the fat. Drain, pat dry on absorbent kitchen paper and leave until cold.

3 Mix together the soy sauce, dark brown sugar and the ½ teaspoon of salt. Rub this mixture generously over the duck legs. Transfer to a wire rack set over a roasting tin and roast in the preheated oven for 30–40 minutes, or until well cooked and the skin is browned and crisp. Remove from the oven and leave to rest for 10 minutes.

4 Shred the duck meat using a fork to hold the hot duck leg and another to remove the meat. Transfer to a warmed serving platter with the cucumber and spring onions. Serve immediately with the plum compote and warmed pancakes.

FOOD FACT

Warm pancakes by stacking and wrapping in tinfoil and placing on a plate in a steamer or for 15 minutes in the oven, after removing the duck and turning the oven off.

1

2

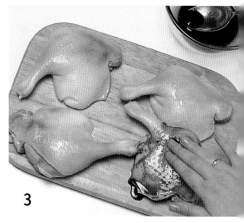

3

Duck in Black Bean Sauce

INGREDIENTS

Serves 4

450 g/1 lb duck breast, skinned
1 tbsp light soy sauce
1 tbsp Chinese rice wine or dry sherry
2.5 cm/1 inch piece fresh root ginger
3 garlic cloves
2 spring onions
2 tbsp Chinese preserved black beans
1 tbsp groundnut or vegetable oil
150 ml/¼ pint chicken stock
shredded spring onions, to garnish
freshly cooked noodles, to serve

HELPFUL HINT

The way in which a dish is presented and garnished is extremely important in both Chinese and Thai cuisine. Fine shreds of colourful vegetables are simple to make. For spring onion shreds, cut off most of the white bulb end and trim the tops. Cut the remaining green part lengthways into fine shreds. These can be curled by dropping them into iced water for a few minutes.

1 Using a sharp knife, trim the duck breasts, removing any fat. Slice thickly and place in a shallow dish. Mix together the soy sauce and Chinese rice wine or sherry and pour over the duck. Leave to marinate for 1 hour in the refrigerator, then drain and discard the marinade.

2 Peel the ginger and chop finely. Peel the garlic cloves and either chop finely or crush. Trim the root from the spring onions, discard the outer leaves and chop. Finely chop the black beans.

3 Heat a wok or large frying pan, add the oil and when very hot, add the ginger, garlic, spring onions and black beans and stir-fry for 30 seconds. Add the drained duck and stir-fry for 3–5 minutes or until the duck is browned.

4 Add the chicken stock to the wok, bring to the boil, then reduce the heat and simmer for 5 minutes, or until the duck is cooked and the sauce is reduced and thickened. Remove from the heat. Tip on to a bed of freshly cooked noodles, garnish with spring onion shreds and serve immediately.

1

3

4

Hoisin Duck & Greens Stir Fry

INGREDIENTS

Serves 4

350 g/12 oz duck breasts, skinned
  and cut into strips
1 medium egg white, beaten
½ tsp salt
1 tsp sesame oil
2 tsp cornflour
2 tbsp groundnut oil
2 tbsp freshly grated root ginger
50 g/2 oz bamboo shoots
50 g/2 oz fine green beans, trimmed
50 g/2 oz pak choi, trimmed
2 tbsp hoisin sauce
1 tsp Chinese rice wine or dry sherry
zest and juice of ½ orange
strips of orange zest, to garnish
freshly steamed egg noodles, to serve

1 Place the duck strips in a shallow dish, then add the egg white, salt, sesame oil and cornflour. Stir lightly until the duck is coated in the mixture. Cover and chill in the refrigerator for 20 minutes.

2 Heat the wok until very hot and add the oil. Remove the wok from the heat and add the duck, stirring continuously to prevent the duck from sticking to the wok. Add the ginger and stir-fry for 2 minutes. Add the bamboo shoots, the green beans and the pak choi, and stir-fry for 1–2 minutes until wilted.

3 Mix together the hoisin sauce, the Chinese rice wine or sherry and the orange zest and juice. Pour into the wok and stir to coat the duck and vegetables. Stir-fry for 1–2 minutes, or until the duck and vegetables are tender. Garnish with the strips of orange zest and serve immediately with freshly steamed egg noodles.

HELPFUL HINT

Duck breasts are usually sold with the skin on, but it is very easy to remove and all the fat usually comes away readily with the skin. If any remains, simply remove with a sharp knife.

1

2

3

Honey-Glazed Duck in Kumquat Sauce

INGREDIENTS

Serves 4

4 duck breast fillets
1 tbsp light soy sauce
1 tsp sesame oil
1 tbsp clear honey
3 tbsp brandy
1 tbsp sunflower oil
2 tbsp caster sugar
1 tbsp white wine vinegar
150 ml/¼ pint orange juice
125 g/4 oz kumquats, thinly sliced
2 tsp cornflour
salt and freshly ground black pepper
fresh watercress, to garnish
basmati and wild rice, to serve

FOOD FACT

Kumquats are tiny citrus fruits that resemble miniature oranges. They have a strong sharp/sweet flavour and are entirely edible, skin and all. They often contain many seeds, so it is worth halving or slicing them before using.

1 Thinly slice the duck breasts and put in a shallow bowl. Mix together the soy sauce, sesame oil, honey and 1 tablespoon of brandy. Pour over the duck, stir well, cover and marinate in the refrigerator for at least 1 hour.

2 Heat a wok until hot, add the sunflower oil and swirl it round to coat the sides. Drain the duck, reserving the marinade, and stir-fry over a high heat for 2–3 minutes, or until browned. Remove from the wok; reserve.

3 Wipe the wok clean with absorbent kitchen paper. Add the sugar, vinegar and 1 tablespoon of water. Gently heat until the sugar dissolves, then boil until a rich golden colour. Pour in the orange juice, then the remaining brandy. Stir in the kumquat slices and simmer for 5 minutes.

4 Blend the cornflour with 1 tablespoon of cold water. Add to the wok and simmer for 2–3 minutes, stirring until thickened. Return the duck to the wok and cook gently for 1–2 minutes, or until warmed through. Season to taste with salt and pepper. Spoon onto warmed plates and garnish with fresh watercress leaves. Serve immediately with freshly cooked basmati and wild rice.

Hot Duck Pasta Salad

INGREDIENTS

Serves 6

3 boneless and skinless duck breasts
1 tbsp wholegrain mustard
1 tbsp clear honey
salt and freshly ground black pepper
4 medium eggs
450 g/1 lb fusilli
125 g/1 oz French beans, trimmed
1 large carrot, peeled and cut into
  thin batons
125 g/4 oz sweetcorn kernels
75 g/3 oz fresh baby spinach
  leaves, shredded

For the dressing:

8 tbsp French dressing
1 tsp horseradish sauce
4 tbsp crème fraîche

HELPFUL HINT

Eggs should never be boiled rapidly as this may make the whites rubbery. When hard-boiling eggs, turn them once or twice in the first few minutes of cooking, so that the yolks stay in the middle. Once cooked, place the eggs in a bowl of very cold water to prevent dark rings forming around the yolks.

1 Preheat the oven to 200°C/400°F/Gas Mark 6. Place the duck breasts on a baking sheet lined with tinfoil. Mix together the wholegrain mustard and honey, season lightly with salt and pepper then spread over the duck breasts. Roast in the preheated oven for 20–30 minutes or until tender. Remove from the oven and keep warm.

2 Meanwhile, place the eggs in a small saucepan, cover with water and bring to the boil. Simmer for 8 minutes, then drain. Bring a large pan of lightly salted water to a rolling boil. Add the beans and pasta, return to the boil and cook according to the packet instructions or until 'al dente'. Drain the pasta and beans and refresh under cold running water.

3 Place the pasta and beans in a bowl, add the carrot, sweetcorn, and spinach leaves, and toss lightly. Shell the eggs, cut into wedges and arrange on top of the pasta. Slice the duck breasts then place them on top of the salad. Beat the dressing ingredients together in a bowl until well blended, then drizzle over the salad. Serve immediately.

Lime & Sesame Turkey

INGREDIENTS

Serves 4

450 g/1 lb turkey breast, skinned and
  cut into strips
2 lemon grass stalks, outer leaves
  discarded and finely sliced
grated zest of 1 lime
4 garlic cloves, peeled and crushed
6 shallots, peeled and finely sliced
2 tbsp Thai fish sauce
2 tsp soft brown sugar
1 small red chilli, deseeded and
  finely sliced
3 tbsp sunflower oil
1 tbsp sesame oil
225 g/8 oz stir-fry rice noodles
1 tbsp sesame seeds
shredded spring onions, to garnish
freshly stir-fried vegetables, to serve

1   Place the turkey strips in a shallow dish. Mix together the lemon grass stalks, lime zest, garlic, shallots, Thai fish sauce, sugar and chilli with 2 tablespoons of the sunflower oil and the sesame oil. Pour over the turkey. Cover and leave to marinate in the refrigerator for 2–3 hours, spooning the marinade over the turkey occasionally.

2   Soak the noodles in warm water for 5 minutes. Drain through a sieve or colander, then plunge immediately into cold water. Drain again and reserve until ready to use.

3   Heat the wok until very hot and add the sesame seeds. Dry-fry for 1–2 minutes, or until toasted in colour. Remove from the wok and reserve. Wipe the wok to remove any dust left from the seeds.

4   Heat the wok again and add the remaining sunflower oil. When hot, drain the turkey from the marinade and stir-fry for 3–4 minutes, or until golden brown and cooked through (you may need to do this in 2 batches). When all the turkey has been cooked, add the noodles to the wok and cook, stirring, for 1–2 minutes, or until heated through thoroughly. Garnish with the shredded spring onions, toasted sesame seeds and serve immediately with freshly stir-fried vegetables of your choice.

FOOD FACT

Lemon grass is a common ingredient in Thai cooking. It looks a little like a spring onion but has a distinctive lemony flavour. It keeps well for 2–3 weeks in the refrigerator.

1

3

4

Noodles with Turkey & Mushrooms

INGREDIENTS

Serves 4

225 g/8 oz dried egg noodles
1 tbsp groundnut oil
1 red onion, peeled and sliced
2 tbsp freshly grated root ginger
3 garlic cloves, peeled and
  finely chopped
350 g/12 oz turkey breast, skinned
  and cut into strips
125 g/4 oz baby button mushrooms
150 g/5 oz chestnut mushrooms
2 tbsp dark soy sauce
2 tbsp hoisin sauce
2 tbsp dry sherry
4 tbsp vegetable stock
2 tsp cornflour

1 Bring a large saucepan of lightly salted water to the boil and add the noodles. Cook for 3–5 minutes, then drain and plunge immediately into cold water. When cool, drain again and reserve.

2 Heat the wok, add the oil and when hot, add the onion and stir-fry for 3 minutes until it starts to soften. Add the ginger and garlic and stir-fry for a further 3 minutes, then add the turkey strips and stir-fry for 4–5 minutes until sealed and golden.

3 Wipe and slice the chestnut mushrooms into similar-sized pieces and add to the wok with the whole button mushrooms. Stir-fry for 3–4 minutes, or until tender. When all the vegetables are tender and the turkey is cooked, add the soy sauce, hoisin sauce, sherry and vegetable stock.

4 Mix the cornflour with 2 tablespoons of water and add to the wok, then cook, stirring, until the sauce thickens. Add the drained noodles to the wok, then toss the mixture together and serve immediately.

HELPFUL HINT

When buying wild mushrooms, choose dry-looking specimens without any soft spots. To prepare them, do not wash but brush away any dirt and wipe over gently with a damp cloth.

Seared Duck with Pickled Plums

INGREDIENTS

Serves 4

4 small skinless, boneless duck breasts

2 garlic cloves, peeled and crushed

1 tsp hot chilli sauce

2 tsp clear honey

2 tsp dark brown sugar

juice of 1 lime

1 tbsp dark soy sauce

6 large plums, halved and
  stones removed

50 g/2 oz caster sugar

50 ml/2 fl oz white wine vinegar

$\frac{1}{4}$ tsp dried chilli flakes

$\frac{1}{4}$ tsp ground cinnamon

1 tbsp sunflower oil

150 ml/$\frac{1}{4}$ pint chicken stock

2 tbsp oyster sauce

sprigs of fresh flat leaf parsley,
  to garnish

freshly cooked noodles, to serve

1 Cut a few deep slashes in each duck breast and place in a shallow dish. Mix together the garlic, chilli sauce, honey, brown sugar, lime juice and soy sauce. Spread over the duck and leave to marinate in the refrigerator for 4 hours or overnight, if time permits, turning occasionally.

2 Place the plums in a saucepan with the caster sugar, white wine vinegar, chilli flakes and cinnamon and bring to the boil. Simmer gently for 5 minutes, or until the plums have just softened, then leave to cool.

3 Remove the duck from the marinade and pat dry with absorbent kitchen paper. Reserve the marinade. Heat a wok or large frying pan, add the oil and when hot, brown the duck on both sides. Pour in the stock, oyster sauce and reserved marinade and simmer for 5 minutes. Remove the duck and keep warm.

4 Remove the plums from their liquid and reserve. Pour the liquid into the duck sauce, bring to the boil, then simmer, uncovered, for 5 minutes, or until reduced and thickened. Arrange the duck on warmed plates. Divide the plums between the plates and spoon over the sauce. Garnish with parsley and serve immediately with noodles.

HELPFUL HINT

When marinating use a glass or glazed earthenware dish. Plastic dishes will absorb the smell and colour of marinades; metal may react with acidic ingredients.

1

3

Shredded Duck in Lettuce Leaves

INGREDIENTS

Serves 4–6

15 g/½ oz dried Chinese
   (shiitake) mushrooms
2 tbsp vegetable oil
400 g/14 oz boneless, skinless duck
   breast, cut crossways into thin strips
1 red chilli, deseeded and diagonally
   thinly sliced
4–6 spring onions, trimmed and
   diagonally sliced
2 garlic cloves, peeled and crushed
75 g/3 oz beansprouts
3 tbsp soy sauce
1 tbsp Chinese rice wine or dry sherry
1–2 tsp clear honey or brown sugar
4–6 tbsp hoisin sauce
large, crisp lettuce leaves such as
   iceberg or cos
handful of fresh mint leaves
sweet chilli dipping sauce

1 Cover the dried Chinese mushrooms with almost boiling water, leave for 20 minutes, then drain and slice thinly.

2 Heat a large wok, add the oil and when hot stir-fry the duck for 3–4 minutes, or until sealed. Remove with a slotted spoon and reserve.

3 Add the chilli, spring onions, garlic and Chinese mushrooms to the wok and stir-fry for 2–3 minutes, or until softened.

4 Add the beansprouts, the soy sauce, Chinese rice wine or dry sherry and honey or brown sugar to the wok, and continue to stir-fry for 1 minute, or until blended.

5 Stir in the reserved duck and stir-fry for 2 minutes, or until well mixed together and heated right through. Transfer to a heated serving dish.

6 Arrange the hoisin sauce in a small bowl on a tray or plate with a pile of lettuce leaves and the mint leaves.

7 Let each guest spoon a little hoisin sauce onto a lettuce leaf, then top with a large spoonful of the stir-fried duck and vegetables and roll up the leaf to enclose the filling. Serve with the dipping sauce.

FOOD FACT

Hoisin sauce is a sweet and spicy aromatic Chinese sauce made primarily from soy beans, sugar, garlic and chilli.

1

4

5

Szechuan Turkey Noodles

INGREDIENTS

Serves 4

1 tbsp tomato paste

2 tsp black bean sauce

2 tsp cider vinegar

salt and freshly ground black pepper

$\frac{1}{2}$ tsp Szechuan pepper

2 tsp sugar

4 tsp sesame oil

225 g/8 oz dried egg noodles

2 tbsp groundnut oil

2 tsp freshly grated root ginger

3 garlic cloves, peeled and
  roughly chopped

2 shallots, peeled and finely chopped

2 courgettes, trimmed and cut into
  fine matchsticks

450 g/1 lb turkey breast, skinned and
  cut into strips

deep-fried onion rings, to garnish

FOOD FACT

Fresh ginger is indispensable in Chinese cookery. It adds a subtle but distinctive flavour to all types of dishes. Root ginger has a gnarled appearance and can vary in size. It has a pale brown, papery skin, usually removed before use. Look for firm pieces with no signs of shrivelling. Keep refrigerated.

1 Mix together the tomato paste, black bean sauce, cider vinegar, a pinch of salt and pepper, the sugar and half the sesame oil. Chill in the refrigerator for 30 minutes.

2 Bring a large saucepan of lightly salted water to the boil and add the noodles. Cook for 3–5 minutes, drain and plunge immediately into cold water. Toss with the remaining sesame oil and reserve.

3 Heat the wok until very hot, then add the oil and when hot, add the ginger, garlic and shallots. Stir-fry for 20 seconds, then add the courgettes and turkey strips. Stir-fry for 3–4 minutes, or until the turkey strips are sealed.

4 Add the prepared chilled black bean sauce and continue to stir-fry for another 4 minutes over a high heat. Add the drained noodles to the wok and stir until the noodles, turkey, vegetables and the sauce are well mixed together. Garnish with the deep-fried onion rings and serve immediately.

1

3

4

Sticky–Glazed Spatchcocked Poussins

INGREDIENTS

Serves 4

2 poussins, each about 700 g/1½ lb
salt and freshly ground black pepper
4 kumquats, thinly sliced
assorted salad leaves, crusty bread or
   new potatoes, to serve

For the glaze:
zest of 1 small lemon, finely grated
1 tbsp lemon juice
1 tbsp dry sherry
2 tbsp clear honey
2 tbsp dark soy sauce
2 tbsp whole-grain mustard
1 tsp tomato purée
½ tsp Chinese five spice powder

1 Preheat the grill just before cooking. Place one of the poussins breast-side down on a board. Using poultry shears, cut down one side of the backbone. Cut down the other side of the backbone. Remove the bone.

2 Open out the poussin and press down hard on the breast bone with the heel of your hand to break it and to flatten the poussin.

3 Thread two skewers crosswise through the bird to keep it flat, ensuring that each skewer goes through a wing and out through the leg on the opposite side. Repeat with the other bird. Season both sides of the bird with salt and pepper.

4 To make the glaze, mix together the lemon zest and juice, sherry, honey, soy sauce, mustard, tomato purée and Chinese five spice powder and use to brush all over the poussins.

5 Place the poussins skin-side down on a grill rack and grill under a medium heat for 15 minutes, brushing halfway through with more glaze.

6 Turn the poussins over and grill for 10 minutes. Brush again with glaze and arrange the kumquat slices on top. Grill for a further 15 minutes until well-browned and cooked through. If they start to brown too quickly, turn down the grill a little.

7 Remove the skewers and cut each poussin in half along the breastbone. Serve immediately with the salad, crusty bread or new potatoes.

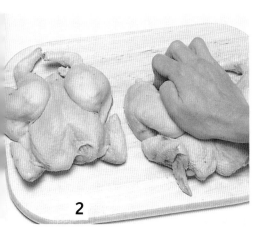

2

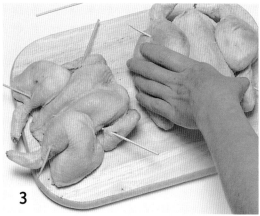

3

6

Sweet-&-Sour Turkey

INGREDIENTS

Serves 4

2 tbsp groundnut oil

2 garlic cloves, peeled and chopped

1 tbsp freshly grated root ginger

4 spring onions, trimmed and cut
into 4 cm/1½ inch lengths

450 g/1 lb turkey breast, skinned and
cut into strips

1 red pepper, deseeded and cut into
2.5 cm/1 inch squares

225 g/8 oz canned water chestnuts

150 ml/¼ pint chicken stock

2 tbsp Chinese rice wine

3 tbsp light soy sauce

2 tsp dark soy sauce

2 tbsp tomato paste

2 tbsp white wine vinegar

1 tbsp sugar

1 tbsp cornflour

egg-fried rice, to serve

TASTY TIP

To make egg-fried rice, stir-fry
450 g/1 lb cooked rice in 1 tbsp
vegetable oil; add 125 g/4 oz
thawed frozen peas and stir-fry for
5 minutes; add 2 beaten eggs and
125 g/4 oz beansprouts and cook
until the eggs have set.

1 Heat the wok over a high heat, add the oil and when hot, add the garlic, ginger and spring onions, stir-fry for 20 seconds.

2 Add the turkey to the wok and stir-fry for 2 minutes, or until beginning to colour. Add the peppers and drained water chestnuts and stir-fry for a further 2 minutes.

3 Mix the chicken stock, Chinese rice wine, light and dark soy sauce, tomato paste, white wine vinegar and the sugar together in a small jug or bowl. Add the mixture to the wok, stir and bring the sauce to the boil.

4 Mix together the cornflour with 2 tablespoons of water and add to the wok. Reduce the heat and simmer for 3 minutes, or until the turkey is cooked thoroughly and the sauce slightly thickened and glossy. Serve immediately with egg-fried rice.

Fried Ginger Rice with Soy Glazed Duck

INGREDIENTS

Serves 4–6

2 duck breasts, skinned and
  diagonally cut into thin slices
2–3 tbsp Japanese soy sauce
1 tbsp mirin (sweet rice wine)
  or sherry
2 tbsp brown sugar
5 cm/2 inch piece of fresh root ginger,
  peeled and finely chopped
4 tbsp peanut or vegetable oil
2 garlic cloves, peeled and crushed
300 g/11 oz long-grain brown rice
900 ml/1½ pints chicken stock
freshly ground black pepper
125 g/4 oz lean ham, diced
175 g/6 oz mangetout, diagonally
  cut in half
8 spring onions, trimmed and
  diagonally thinly sliced
1 tbsp freshly chopped coriander
sweet or hot chilli sauce, to taste
  (optional)
sprigs of fresh coriander, to garnish

1   Put the duck slices in a bowl with 1 tablespoon of the soy sauce, the mirin, 1 teaspoon of the sugar and one-third of the ginger; stir. Leave to stand.

2   Heat 2 tablespoons of the oil in a large heavy-based saucepan. Add the garlic and half the remaining ginger and stir-fry for 1 minute. Add the rice and cook for 3 minutes, stirring constantly, until translucent.

3   Stir in all but 125 ml/4 fl oz of the stock, with 1 teaspoon of the soy sauce, and bring to the boil. Season with pepper. Reduce the heat to very low and simmer, covered, for 25–30 minutes until the rice is tender and the liquid is absorbed. Cover and leave to stand.

4   Heat the remaining oil in a large frying pan or wok. Drain the duck strips and add to the frying pan. Stir-fry for 2–3 minutes until just coloured. Add 1 tablespoon of soy sauce and the remaining sugar and cook for 1 minute until glazed. Transfer to a plate and keep warm.

5   Stir in the ham, mangetout, spring onions, the remaining ginger and the chopped coriander. Add the remaining stock and duck marinade and cook until the liquid is almost reduced. Fork in the rice and a little chilli sauce to taste (if using); stir well. Turn into a serving dish and top with the duck. Garnish with coriander sprigs and serve immediately.

1

3

4

Chef's Rice Salad

INGREDIENTS

Serves 4

225 g/8 oz wild rice
½ cucumber
175 g/6 oz cherry tomatoes
6 spring onions, trimmed
5 tbsp extra virgin olive oil
2 tbsp balsamic vinegar
1 tsp Dijon mustard
1 tsp caster sugar
salt and freshly ground black pepper
125 g/4 oz rocket
125 g/4 oz back bacon
125 g/4 oz cooked chicken meat,
  finely diced
125 g/4 oz Emmenthal cheese, grated
125 g/4 oz large cooked prawns,
  peeled
1 avocado, stoned, peeled and sliced,
  to garnish
warm crusty bread, to serve

TASTY TIP

You can use any combination of cold meats in this salad; smoked duck or chicken works particularly well. Emmenthal cheese has a mellow and sweet flavour that is good in this salad, or you can use hard cheeses such as Jarlsberg, Gouda or Gruyère.

1 Put the rice in in a saucepan of water and bring to the boil, stirring once or twice. Reduce the heat, cover and simmer gently for 30–50 minutes, depending on the texture you prefer. Drain well and reserve.

2 Thinly peel the cucumber, cut in half, then using a teaspoon, remove the seeds. Cut the cucumber into thin slices. Cut the tomatoes in quarters. Cut the spring onions into diagonal slices.

3 Whisk the olive oil with the vinegar, then whisk in the mustard and sugar. Season to taste with salt and pepper.

4 In a large bowl, gently toss together the cooled rice with the tomatoes, cucumber, spring onions and the rocket. Pour over the dressing and toss lightly together.

5 Heat a griddle pan and when hot cook the bacon on both sides for 4–6 minutes, or until crisp. Remove and chop. Arrange the prepared rocket salad on a platter, then arrange the bacon, chicken, cheese and prawns on top. Toss, if wished. Garnish with avocado slices and serve with plenty of warm, crusty bread.

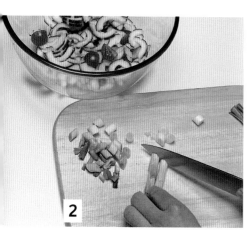

2

3

5

Chicken & Baby Vegetable Stir Fry

INGREDIENTS

Serves 4

2 tbsp groundnut oil

1 small red chilli, deseeded and
  finely chopped

150 g/5 oz chicken breast or thigh
  meat, skinned and cut into cubes

2 baby leeks, trimmed and sliced

12 asparagus spears, halved

125 g/4 oz mangetout peas, trimmed

125 g/4 oz baby carrots, trimmed and
  halved lengthways

125 g/4 oz fine green beans, trimmed
  and diagonally sliced

125 g/4 oz baby sweetcorn,
  diagonally halved

50 ml/2 fl oz chicken stock

2 tsp light soy sauce

1 tbsp dry sherry

1 tsp sesame oil

toasted sesame seeds, to garnish

1   Heat the wok until very hot and add the oil. Add the chopped chilli and chicken and stir-fry for 4–5 minutes, or until the chicken is cooked and golden.

2   Increase the heat, add the leeks to the chicken and stir-fry for 2 minutes. Add the asparagus spears, mangetout peas, baby carrots, green beans, and baby sweetcorn. Stir-fry for 3–4 minutes, or until the vegetables soften slightly but still retain a slight crispness.

3   In a small bowl, mix together the chicken stock, soy sauce, dry sherry and sesame oil. Pour into the wok, stir and cook until heated through. Sprinkle with the toasted sesame seeds and serve immediately.

HELPFUL HINT

Look for packs of mixed baby vegetables in the supermarket. They are often available ready-trimmed and will save a lot of time.

1

2

3

Chicken & Cashew Nuts

INGREDIENTS

Serves 4

450 g/1 lb skinless chicken,
  boneless breast fillets, cut into
  1 cm/½ inch cubes
1 medium egg white, beaten
1 tsp salt
1 tsp sesame oil
2 tsp cornflour
300 ml/½ pint groundnut oil for
  deep frying
2 tsp sunflower oil
50 g/2 oz unsalted cashews
4 spring onions, shredded
50 g/2 oz mangetout peas,
  diagonally sliced
1 tbsp Chinese rice wine
1 tbsp light soy sauce
shredded spring onions, to garnish
freshly steamed white rice with fresh
  coriander leaves, to serve

1 Place the cubes of chicken in a large bowl. Add the egg white, salt, sesame oil and cornflour. Mix well to ensure the chicken is coated thoroughly. Chill in the refrigerator for 20 minutes.

2 Heat the wok until very hot, add the groundnut oil and when hot, remove the wok from the heat and add the chicken. Stir continuously to prevent the chicken from sticking to the wok. When the chicken turns white, after about 2 minutes, remove it using a slotted spoon and reserve. Discard the oil.

3 Wipe the wok clean with absorbent kitchen paper and heat it again until very hot. Add the sunflower oil and heat. When hot, add the cashew nuts, spring onions and mangetout peas and stir-fry for 1 minute.

4 Add the rice wine and soy sauce. Return the chicken to the wok and stir-fry for 2 minutes. Garnish with shredded spring onions and serve immediately with freshly steamed rice sprinkled with fresh coriander.

1

2

3

Chicken & Red Pepper Curried Rice

INGREDIENTS

Serves 4

350 g/12 oz long-grain rice
salt
1 large egg white
1 tbsp cornflour
300 g/11 oz skinless chicken breast
   fillets, cut into chunks
3 tbsp groundnut oil
1 red pepper, deseeded and
   roughly chopped
1 tbsp curry powder or paste
125 ml/4 fl oz chicken stock
1 tsp sugar
1 tbsp Chinese rice wine or dry sherry
1 tbsp light soy sauce
sprigs of fresh coriander, to garnish

1 Wash the rice in several changes of water until the water remains relatively clear. Drain well. Put into a saucepan and cover with fresh water. Add a little salt and bring to the boil. Cook for 7–8 minutes until tender. Drain and refresh under cold running water, then drain again and reserve.

2 Lightly whisk the egg white with 1 teaspoon of salt and 2 teaspoons of cornflour until smooth. Add the chicken and mix together well. Cover and chill in the refrigerator for 20 minutes.

3 Heat the oil in a wok until moderately hot. Add the chicken mixture to the wok and stir-fry for 2–3 minutes until all the chicken has turned white. Using a slotted spoon, lift the cubes of chicken from the wok, then drain on absorbent kitchen paper.

4 Add the red peppers to the wok and stir-fry for 1 minute over a high heat. Add the curry powder or paste and cook for a further 30 seconds, then add the chicken stock, sugar, Chinese rice wine and soy sauce.

5 Mix the remaining cornflour with 1 teaspoon of cold water and add to the wok, stirring. Bring to the boil and simmer gently for 1 minute.

6 Return the chicken to the wok, then simmer for a further 1 minute before adding the rice. Stir over a medium heat for another 2 minutes until heated through. Garnish with the sprigs of coriander and serve.

2

4

6

Chicken Chow Mein

INGREDIENTS

Serves 4

225 g/8 oz egg noodles

5 tsp sesame oil

4 tsp light soy sauce

2 tbsp Chinese rice wine or dry sherry

salt and freshly ground black pepper

225 g/8 oz skinless chicken breast
fillets, cut into strips

3 tbsp groundnut oil

2 garlic cloves, peeled and
finely chopped

50 g/2 oz mangetout peas,
finely sliced

50 g/2 oz cooked ham, cut into
fine strips

2 tsp dark soy sauce

pinch of sugar

To garnish:

shredded spring onions

toasted sesame seeds

FOOD FACT

Sesame oil is a thick, rich, golden brown oil made from toasted sesame seeds. It is used in Chinese cooking mainly as a seasoning.

1 Bring a large saucepan of water to the boil and add the noodles. Cook for 3–5 minutes, drain and plunge into cold water. Drain again, add 1 tablespoon of the sesame oil and stir lightly.

2 Place 2 teaspoons of light soy sauce, 1 tablespoon of Chinese rice wine or sherry, and 1 teaspoon of the sesame oil, with seasoning to taste in a bowl. Add the chicken and stir well. Cover lightly and leave to marinate in the refrigerator for about 15 minutes.

3 Heat the wok over a high heat, add 1 tablespoon of the groundnut oil and when very hot, add the chicken and its marinade and stir-fry for 2 minutes. Remove the chicken and juices and reserve. Wipe the wok clean with absorbent kitchen paper.

4 Reheat the wok and add the oil. Add the garlic and toss in the oil for 20 seconds. Add the mangetout peas and the ham and stir-fry for 1 minute. Add the noodles, remaining light soy sauce, Chinese rice wine or sherry, the dark soy sauce and sugar. Season to taste with salt and pepper and stir-fry for 2 minutes.

5 Add the chicken and juices to the wok and stir-fry for 4 minutes, or until the chicken is cooked. Drizzle over the remaining sesame oil. Garnish with spring onions and sesame seeds and serve.

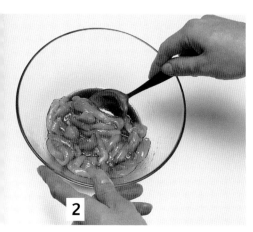

2

4

5

Chicken in Black Bean Sauce

INGREDIENTS

Serves 4

450 g/1 lb skinless, boneless chicken
  breast fillets, cut into strips
1 tbsp light soy sauce
2 tbsp Chinese rice wine or dry sherry
salt
1 tsp caster sugar
1 tsp sesame oil
2 tsp cornflour
2 tbsp sunflower oil
2 green peppers, deseeded and diced
1 tbsp freshly grated root ginger
2 garlic cloves, peeled and
  roughly chopped
2 shallots, peeled and finely chopped
4 spring onions, trimmed and
  finely sliced
3 tbsp salted black beans, chopped
150 ml/¼ pint chicken stock
shredded spring onions, to garnish
freshly cooked egg noodles,
  to serve

1. Place the chicken strips in a large bowl. Mix together the soy sauce, Chinese rice wine or sherry, a little salt, caster sugar, sesame oil and cornflour and pour over the chicken.

2. Heat the wok over a high heat, add the oil and when very hot, add the chicken strips and stir-fry for 2 minutes. Add the green peppers and stir-fry for a further 2 minutes. Then add the ginger, garlic, shallots, spring onions and black beans and continue to stir-fry for another 2 minutes.

3. Add 4 tablespoons of the stock, stir-fry for 1 minute, then pour in the remaining stock and bring to the boil. Reduce the heat and simmer the sauce for 3–4 minutes, or until the chicken is cooked and the sauce has thickened slightly. Garnish with the shredded spring onions and serve immediately with noodles.

1

2

3

Chicken with Noodles

INGREDIENTS

Serves 2–3

225 g/8 oz medium egg noodles

125 g/4 oz skinless, boneless chicken
    breast fillets

1 tbsp light soy sauce

2 tsp Chinese rice wine or dry sherry

5 tsp groundnut oil

2 garlic cloves, peeled and
    finely chopped

50 g/2 oz mangetout peas

25 g/1 oz smoked back bacon, cut
    into fine strips

½ tsp sugar

2 spring onions, peeled and
    finely chopped

1 tsp sesame oil

1 Cook the noodles according to the packet directions. Drain and refresh under cold water. Drain again and reserve.

2 Slice the chicken into fine shreds and mix with 2 teaspoons of the light soy sauce and Chinese rice wine. Leave to marinate in the refrigerator for 10 minutes.

3 Heat a wok, add 2 teaspoons of the oil and when hot, stir-fry the chicken shreds for about 2 minutes, then transfer to a plate. Wipe the wok clean with absorbent kitchen paper.

4 Return the wok to the heat and add the remaining oil. Add the garlic, then after 10 seconds add the mangetout peas and bacon. Stir-fry for a further 1 minute, then add the drained noodles, remaining soy sauce, sugar and spring onions. Stir-fry for a further 2 minutes then add the reserved chicken.

5 Stir-fry for a further 3–4 minutes until the chicken is cooked through. Add the sesame oil and mix together. Serve either hot or cold.

FOOD FACT

Chow mein literally means 'stir-fried noodles'. There are no hard and fast rules about which meat, fish or vegetables can be used. Chow mein also makes a tasty salad if served cold.

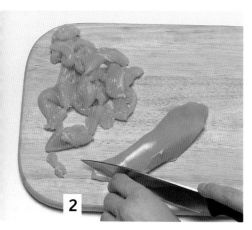

2

3

4

Chinese–Style Fried Rice

INGREDIENTS

Serves 4–6

2–3 tbsp groundnut oil or vegetable oil

2 small onions, peeled and cut
   into wedges

2 garlic cloves, peeled and thinly sliced

2.5 cm/1 inch piece of fresh root ginger,
   peeled and cut into thin slivers

225 g/8 oz cooked chicken,
   thinly sliced

125 g/4 oz cooked ham, thinly sliced

350 g/12 oz cooked cold long-grain
   white rice

125 g/4 oz canned water
   chestnuts, sliced

225 g/8 oz cooked peeled prawns
   (optional)

3 large eggs

3 tsp sesame oil

salt and freshly ground black pepper

6 spring onions, trimmed and sliced
   into 1 cm/½ inch pieces

2 tbsp dark soy sauce

1 tbsp sweet chilli sauce

2 tbsp freshly chopped coriander

To garnish:

2 tbsp chopped roasted peanuts

sprig of fresh coriander

1 Heat a wok or large deep frying pan until very hot, add the oil and heat for 30 seconds. Add the onions and stir-fry for 2 minutes. Stir in the garlic and ginger and cook for 1 minute. Add the cooked sliced chicken and ham and stir-fry for a further 2–3 minutes.

2 Add the rice, the water chestnuts and prawns, if using, with 2 tablespoons of water, and stir-fry for 2 minutes until the rice is heated through.

3 Beat the eggs with 1 teaspoon of the sesame oil and season to taste with salt and pepper. Make a well in the centre of the rice, then pour in the egg mixture and stir immediately, gradually drawing the rice mixture into the egg, until the egg is cooked.

4 Add the spring onions, soy and chilli sauces, coriander and a little water, if necessary. Adjust the seasoning and drizzle with the remaining sesame oil. Sprinkle with the nuts and serve.

Deep-Fried Chicken Wings

INGREDIENTS

Serves 4

2 tsp turmeric

1 tsp hot chilli powder

1 tsp ground coriander

1 tsp ground cumin

3 garlic cloves, peeled and crushed

8 chicken wings

2 tbsp orange marmalade

2 tbsp ginger preserve or marmalade

1 tsp salt

3 tbsp rice wine vinegar

2 tbsp tomato ketchup

1 litre/1¾ pints vegetable oil for
deep frying

lime wedges, to garnish

HELPFUL HINT

It is important to test the oil to make sure it is at the right temperature. If the oil is not hot enough, the chicken will be greasy but if it is too hot, the food may burn without being properly cooked through.

1 Blend the turmeric, chilli powder, ground coriander, ground cumin and garlic together in a small bowl. Dry the chicken wings thoroughly, using absorbent kitchen paper, then rub the spice mixture onto the skin of each chicken wing. Cover and chill in the refrigerator for at least 2 hours.

2 Meanwhile make the dipping sauce, by mixing together the marmalade, ginger preserve, salt, rice wine vinegar and tomato ketchup in a small saucepan. Heat until blended, leave to cool, then serve. If using straight away, spoon into a small dipping bowl, but if using later pour into a container with a close-fitting lid and store in the refrigerator.

3 Pour the oil into the wok and heat to 190°C/375°F, or until a small cube of bread dropped in the oil turns golden brown in 30 seconds. Cook 2–3 chicken wings at a time, lowering them into the hot oil, and frying for 3–4 minutes. Remove the wings, using a slotted spoon, and drain on absorbent kitchen paper. You may need to reheat the oil before cooking each batch.

4 When all the chicken wings are cooked, arrange on a warmed serving dish, garnish with the lime wedges and serve.

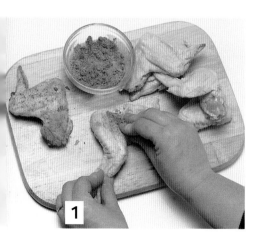

1

2

3

Green Chicken Curry

INGREDIENTS

Serves 4

1 onion, peeled and chopped

3 lemon grass stalks, outer leaves
  discarded and finely sliced

2 garlic cloves, peeled and
  finely chopped

1 tbsp freshly grated root ginger

3 green chillies

zest and juice of 1 lime

2 tbsp groundnut oil

2 tbsp Thai fish sauce

6 tbsp freshly chopped coriander

6 tbsp freshly chopped basil

450 g/1 lb skinless, boneless chicken
  breasts, cut into strips

125 g /4 oz fine green beans, trimmed

400 ml can coconut milk

fresh basil leaves, to garnish

freshly cooked rice, to serve

TASTY TIP

Use Thai holy basil in this recipe if possible. The leaves are flatter and coarser than Italian basil with a stronger, more pronounced aniseed flavour. Thai basil is available from Oriental grocers and some supermarkets.

1 Place the onion, lemon grass, garlic, ginger, chillies, lime zest and juice, 1 tablespoon of groundnut oil, the fish sauce, coriander and basil in a food processor. Blend to a form a smooth paste, which should be of a spoonable consistency. If the sauce looks thick, add a little water. Remove and reserve.

2 Heat the wok, add the remaining 1 tablespoon of oil and when hot add the chicken. Stir-fry for 2–3 minutes, until the chicken starts to colour, then add the green beans and stir-fry for a further minute. Remove the chicken and beans from the wok and reserve. Wipe the wok clean with absorbent kitchen paper.

3 Spoon the reserved green paste into the wok and heat for 1 minute. Add the coconut milk and whisk to blend. Return the chicken and beans to the wok and bring to the boil. Simmer for 5–7 minutes, or until the chicken is cooked. Sprinkle with basil leaves and serve immediately with freshly cooked rice.

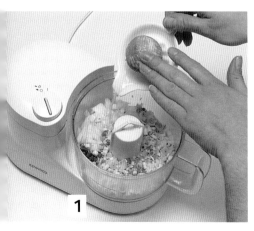

Green Turkey Curry

INGREDIENTS

Serves 4

4 baby aubergines, trimmed
  and quartered
1 tsp salt
2 tbsp sunflower oil
4 shallots, peeled and halved or
  quartered if large
2 garlic cloves, peeled and sliced
2 tbsp Thai green curry paste
150 ml/¼ pint chicken stock
1 tbsp Thai fish sauce
1 tbsp lemon juice
350 g/12 oz boneless, skinless turkey
  breast, cubed
1 red pepper, deseeded and sliced
125 g/4 oz French beans, trimmed
  and halved
25 g/1 oz creamed coconut
freshly boiled rice or steamed Thai
  fragrant rice, to serve

FOOD FACT

Several types of aubergine are grown in Thailand. Generally the Thais prefer the small, thin varieties, which have a more delicate flavour. You may find these in Oriental shops labelled as Chinese aubergines.

1 Place the aubergines into a colander and sprinkle with the salt. Set over a plate or in the sink to drain and leave for 30 minutes. Rinse under cold running water and pat dry on absorbent kitchen paper.

2 Heat a wok or large frying pan, add the sunflower oil and when hot, add the shallots and garlic and stir-fry for 3 minutes, or until beginning to brown. Add the curry paste and stir-fry for 1–2 minutes. Pour in the stock, fish sauce and lemon juice and simmer for 10 minutes.

3 Add the turkey, red pepper and French beans to the wok with the aubergines. Return to the boil, then simmer for 10–15 minutes, or until the turkey and vegetables are tender. Add the creamed coconut and stir until melted and the sauce has thickened. Turn into a warmed serving dish and serve immediately with rice.

1

2

3

Lemon Chicken

INGREDIENTS

Serves 4

450 g/1 lb skinless, boneless chicken
  breast fillets, cubed
1 medium egg white, beaten
1 tsp salt
1 tbsp sesame oil
1 tbsp cornflour
200 ml/7 fl oz groundnut oil
75 ml/3 fl oz chicken stock
zest and juice of 1 lemon
1 tbsp caster sugar
1 tbsp light soy sauce
2 tbsp Chinese rice wine or dry sherry
3 large garlic cloves, peeled and
  finely chopped
1–2 tsp dried red chillies, crushed
shredded fresh red chillies, to garnish
freshly steamed white rice, to serve

1 Place the cubes of chicken in a large bowl then add the beaten egg white, salt, 1 teaspoon of sesame oil and 1 teaspoon of cornflour. Mix lightly together until all the chicken is coated, then chill in the refrigerator for 20 minutes.

2 Heat the wok until very hot and add the oil. When hot, remove the wok from the heat and add the chicken. Stir-fry for 2 minutes, or until the chicken turns white, then remove with a slotted spoon and drain on absorbent kitchen paper.

3 Wipe the wok clean and heat it until hot again. Add the stock, lemon zest and juice, sugar, soy sauce, Chinese rice wine or sherry, garlic and crushed chillies and bring to the boil. Blend the remaining cornflour to a smooth paste with 1 tablespoon of water and add to the wok. Stir, then simmer for 1 minute. Add the chicken cubes and stir-fry for 2–3 minutes. Add the remaining sesame oil, garnish with shredded chillies and serve immediately with freshly steamed rice.

HELPFUL HINT

If possible, use unwaxed lemons for this dish and for any dish using lemon zest. If these are unavailable, pour hot water over the lemons, then scrub them to remove the wax.

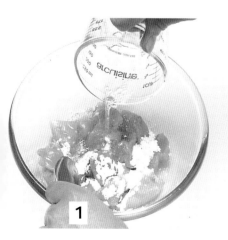

Pad Thai

INGREDIENTS

Serves 4

225 g/8 oz flat rice noodles
2 tbsp vegetable oil
225 g/8 oz boneless chicken breast,
   skinned and thinly sliced
4 shallots, peeled and thinly sliced
2 garlic cloves, peeled and
   finely chopped
4 spring onions, trimmed and
   diagonally cut into 5 cm/2
   inch pieces
350 g/12 oz fresh white crab meat or
   tiny prawns
75 g/3 oz fresh bean sprouts, rinsed
   and drained
2 tbsp preserved or fresh
   radish, chopped
2–3 tbsp roasted peanuts, chopped
   (optional)

For the sauce:

3 tbsp Thai fish sauce (nam pla)
2–3 tbsp rice vinegar or cider vinegar
1 tbsp chilli bean or oyster sauce
1 tbsp toasted sesame oil
1 tbsp light brown sugar
1 red chilli, deseeded and thinly sliced

1 To make the sauce, whisk all the sauce ingredients in a bowl and reserve. Put the rice noodles in a large bowl and pour over enough hot water to cover. Leave to stand for about 15 minutes until softened. Drain and rinse, then drain again.

2 Heat the oil in a wok over a high heat until hot, but not smoking. Add the chicken strips and stir-fry constantly until they begin to colour. Using a slotted spoon, transfer to a plate. Reduce the heat to medium-high.

3 Add the shallots, garlic and spring onions and stir-fry for 1 minute. Stir in the rice noodles, then the reserved sauce; mix well.

4 Add the reserved chicken strips, with the crab meat or prawns, bean sprouts and radish and stir well. Cook for about 5 minutes, stirring frequently, until heated through. If the noodles begin to stick, add a little water.

5 Turn into a large shallow serving dish and sprinkle with the chopped peanuts, if desired. Serve immediately.

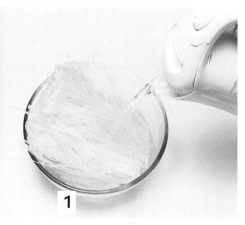

Red Chicken Curry

INGREDIENTS

Serves 4

225 ml/8 fl oz coconut cream
2 tbsp vegetable oil
2 garlic clove, peeled and
   finely chopped
2 tbsp Thai red curry paste
2 tbsp Thai fish sauce
2 tsp sugar
350 g/12 oz boneless, skinless
   chicken breast, finely sliced
450 ml/ ¾ pint chicken stock
2 lime leaves, shredded
chopped red chilli, to garnish
freshly boiled rice or steamed Thai
   fragrant rice, to serve

TASTY TIP

For 4 people, rinse 400 ml/14 fl oz rice under cold, running water and place in 600 ml/1 pint cold water. Add a large pinch of salt, bring to the boil and simmer for 15 minutes, or until most of the water has evaporated. Cover with a tight-fitting lid and cook on as low a heat as possible for a further 5 minutes, or until the rice is tender.

1 Pour the coconut cream into a small saucepan and heat gently. Meanwhile, heat a wok or large frying pan and add the oil. When the oil is very hot, swirl the oil around the wok until the wok is lightly coated, then add the garlic and stir-fry for about 10–20 seconds, or until the garlic begins to brown. Add the curry paste and stir-fry for a few more seconds, then pour in the warmed coconut cream.

2 Cook the coconut cream mixture for 5 minutes, or until the cream has curdled and thickened. Stir in the fish sauce and sugar. Add the finely sliced chicken breast and cook for 3–4 minutes, or until the chicken has turned white.

3 Pour the stock into the wok, bring to the boil, then simmer for 1–2 minutes, or until the chicken is cooked through. Stir in the shredded lime leaves. Turn into a warmed serving dish, garnish with chopped red chilli and serve immediately with rice.

Soy-Glazed Chicken Thighs

INGREDIENTS

Serves 6–8

900 g/2 lb chicken thighs
2 tbsp vegetable oil
3–4 garlic cloves, peeled and crushed
4 cm/1½ inch piece fresh root ginger,
   peeled and finely chopped or grated
125 ml/4 fl oz soy sauce
2–3 tbsp Chinese rice wine or
   dry sherry
2 tbsp clear honey
1 tbsp soft brown sugar
2–3 dashes hot chilli sauce,
   or to taste
freshly chopped parsley, to garnish

1 Heat a large wok and when hot add the oil and heat. Stir-fry the chicken thighs for 5 minutes or until golden. Remove and drain on absorbent kitchen paper. You may need to do this in 2–3 batches.

2 Pour off the oil and fat and, using absorbent kitchen paper, carefully wipe out the wok. Add the garlic, with the root ginger, soy sauce, Chinese rice wine or sherry and honey to the wok and stir well. Sprinkle in the soft brown sugar with the hot chilli sauce to taste, then place over the heat and bring to the boil.

3 Reduce the heat to a gentle simmer, then carefully add the chicken thighs. Cover the wok and simmer gently over a very low heat for 30 minutes, or until they are tender and the sauce is reduced and thickened and glazes the chicken thighs.

4 Stir or spoon the sauce occasionally over the chicken thighs and add a little water if the sauce is starting to become too thick. Arrange in a shallow serving dish, garnish with freshly chopped parsley and serve immediately.

TASTY TIP

Often overlooked, chicken wings are inexpensive and very flavourful. Served this way, with a sticky coating, they make an ideal snack. Serve with finger bowls.

Special Fried Rice

INGREDIENTS

Serves 4

1 large egg

1 tsp sesame oil

350 g/8 oz long-grain white rice

1 tbsp groundnut oil

450 g/1 lb boneless, skinless chicken
  breast, diced

8 spring onions, trimmed and sliced

2 large carrots, trimmed and cut
  into matchsticks

125 g/4 oz sugar snap peas

125 g/4 oz raw tiger prawns, peeled

2 tsp Chinese five spice powder

1 tbsp soy sauce

1 tbsp Thai fish sauce

1 tbsp rice wine vinegar

FOOD FACT

A classic Chinese ingredient, sesame oil is richly coloured and strongly flavoured. It has a low smoking temperature, so should not be heated to an extremely high temperature, otherwise the delicious sesame flavour will be lost.

1 Beat the egg in a bowl with ½ teaspoon of the sesame oil and 2 teaspoons of water. Heat a frying pan over a medium-high heat and swirl in 2 tablespoons of the egg mixture to form a paper-thin omelette. Remove and reserve. Repeat this process until all the egg has been used.

2 Cook the rice in lightly salted boiling water for 12 minutes, or until tender. Drain and reserve.

3 Heat a wok, then add the remaining sesame oil with the groundnut oil and stir-fry the chicken for 5 minutes until cooked through. Using a slotted spoon, remove from the wok and keep warm.

4 Add the spring onions, carrot and sugar snap peas to the wok and stir-fry for 2–3 minutes. Add the prawns and stir-fry for 2–3 minutes, or until pink. Return the chicken to the wok with the Chinese five spice powder and stir-fry for 1 minute. Stir in the drained rice.

5 Mix together the soy sauce, fish sauce and vinegar. Pour into the wok and continue to stir-fry for 2–3 minutes. Roll the papery omelettes into tight rolls and slice to form thin strips. Stir into the rice and serve immediately.

1

4

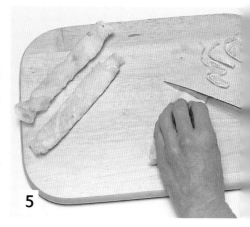

5

Stir–Fried Chicken with Basil

INGREDIENTS

Serves 4

3 tbsp sunflower oil

3 tbsp green curry paste

450 g/1 lb skinless, boneless chicken
    breast fillets, trimmed and cut
    into cubes

8 cherry tomatoes

100 ml/4 fl oz coconut cream

2 tbsp soft brown sugar

2 tbsp Thai fish sauce

1 red chilli, deseeded and thinly sliced

1 green chilli, deseeded and
    thinly sliced

75 g/3 oz fresh torn basil leaves

sprigs of fresh coriander, to garnish

freshly steamed white rice,
    to serve

1 Heat the wok, then add the oil and heat for 1 minute. Add the green curry paste and cook, stirring for 1 minute to release the flavour and cook the paste. Add the chicken and stir-fry over a high heat for 2 minutes, making sure the chicken is coated thoroughly with the green curry paste.

2 Reduce the heat under the wok, then add the cherry tomatoes and cook, stirring gently, for 2–3 minutes, or until the tomatoes burst and begin to disintegrate into the green curry paste.

3 Add half the coconut cream and add to the wok with the brown sugar, Thai fish sauce and the red and green chillies. Stir-fry gently for 5 minutes, or until the sauce is amalgamated and the chicken is cooked thoroughly.

4 Just before serving, sprinkle the chicken with the torn basil leaves and add the remaining coconut cream, then serve immediately with freshly steamed white rice garnished with fresh coriander sprigs.

FOOD FACT

Creamed coconut is a waxy block of hardened coconut cream. It is very high in fat but adds a rich creaminess to the dish. It can be chopped or grated and melts very easily on contact with the hot sauce.

Stir–Fried Chicken with Spinach, Tomatoes & Pine Nuts

INGREDIENTS

Serves 4

50 g/2 oz pine nuts

2 tbsp sunflower oil

1 red onion, peeled and
  finely chopped

450 g/1 lb skinless, boneless chicken
  breast fillets, cut into strips

450 g/1 lb cherry tomatoes, halved

225 g/8 oz baby spinach, washed

salt and freshly ground black pepper

1/4 tsp freshly grated nutmeg

2 tbsp balsamic vinegar

50 g/2 oz raisins

freshly cooked ribbon noodles tossed
  in butter, to serve

1 Heat the wok and add the pine nuts. Dry-fry for about 2 minutes, shaking often to ensure that they toast but do not burn. Remove and reserve. Wipe any dust from the wok.

2 Heat the wok again, add the oil and when hot, add the red onion and stir-fry for 2 minutes. Add the chicken and stir-fry for 2–3 minutes, or until golden brown. Reduce the heat, toss in the cherry tomatoes and stir-fry gently until the tomatoes start to disintegrate.

3 Add the baby spinach and stir-fry for 2–3 minutes, or until they start to wilt. Season to taste with salt and pepper, then sprinkle in the grated nutmeg and drizzle in the balsamic vinegar. Finally, stir in the raisins and reserved toasted pine nuts. Serve immediately on a bed of buttered ribbon noodles.

HELPFUL HINT

Baby spinach is available ready to use in bags, sold in most supermarkets. It has a more subtle, creamier flavour than larger-leaved spinach and cooks very quickly.

Sweet & Sour Rice with Chicken

INGREDIENTS

Serves 4

4 spring onions
2 tsp sesame oil
1 tsp Chinese five spice powder
450 g/1 lb chicken breast,
   cut into cubes
1 tbsp oil
1 garlic clove, peeled and crushed
1 medium onion, peeled and sliced
   into thin wedges
225 g/8 oz long-grain white rice
600 ml/1 pint water
4 tbsp tomato ketchup
1 tbsp tomato purée
2 tbsp honey
1 tbsp vinegar
1 tbsp dark soy sauce
1 carrot, peeled and cut
   into matchsticks

FOOD FACT

Five spice powder is a popular Chinese seasoning that can be bought ready-blended in jars in most supermarkets. It is a mixture of finely ground star anise, fennel, cinnamon, cloves and Szechuan pepper and adds a unique sweet and spicy aniseed flavour to food.

1 Trim the spring onions, then cut lengthways into fine strips. Drop into a large bowl of iced water and reserve.

2 Mix together the sesame oil and Chinese five spice powder and use to rub into the cubed chicken. Heat the wok, then add the oil and when hot, cook the garlic and onion for 2–3 minutes, or until transparent and softened.

3 Add the chicken and stir-fry over a medium-high heat until the chicken is golden and cooked through. Using a slotted spoon, remove from the wok and keep warm.

4 Stir the rice into the wok and add the water, tomato ketchup, tomato purée, honey, vinegar and soy sauce. Stir well to mix. Bring to the boil, then simmer until almost all of the liquid is absorbed. Stir in the carrot and reserved chicken and continue to cook for 3–4 minutes.

5 Drain the spring onions, which will have become curly. Garnish with the spring onion curls and serve immediately with the rice and chicken.

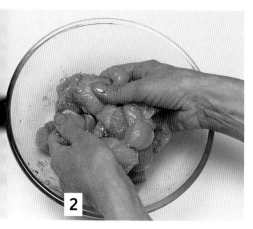

Thai Chicken Fried Rice

INGREDIENTS

Serves 4

175 g/6 oz boneless, chicken breast
2 tbsp vegetable oil
2 garlic cloves, peeled and
   finely chopped
2 tsp medium curry paste
450 g/1 lb cold, cooked rice
1 tbsp light soy sauce
2 tbsp Thai fish sauce
large pinch of sugar
freshly ground black pepper

To garnish:

2 spring onions, trimmed and
   shredded lengthways
½ small onion, peeled and very
   finely sliced

TASTY TIP

There is a huge range of curry pastes available, from mild and only slightly spicy to burning hot. Although a medium one has been suggested for this dish, you can, of course, use your favourite, but do choose a Thai curry paste, such as red or green curry paste, rather than an Indian-style one.

1 Using a sharp knife, trim the chicken, discarding any sinew or fat and cut into small cubes. Reserve.

2 Heat a wok or large frying pan, add the oil and when hot, add the garlic and cook for 10–20 seconds or until just golden. Add the curry paste and stir-fry for a few seconds. Add the chicken and stir-fry for 3–4 minutes, or until tender and the chicken has turned white.

3 Stir the cold, cooked rice into the chicken mixture, then add the soy sauce, fish sauce and sugar, stirring well after each addition. Stir-fry for 2–3 minutes, or until the chicken is cooked through and the rice is piping hot.

4 Check the seasoning and, if necessary, add a little extra soy sauce. Turn the rice and chicken mixture into a warmed serving dish. Season lightly with black pepper and garnish with shredded spring onion and onion slices. Serve immediately.

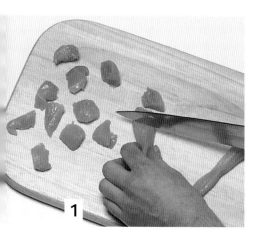

1

2

3

Thai Coconut Chicken

INGREDIENTS

Serves 4

1 tsp cumin seeds
1 tsp mustard seeds
1 tsp coriander seeds
1 tsp turmeric
1 bird's eye chilli, deseeded and
  finely chopped
1 tbsp freshly grated root ginger
2 garlic cloves, peeled and
  finely chopped
125 ml/4 fl oz double cream
8 skinless chicken thighs
2 tbsp groundnut oil
1 onion, peeled and finely sliced
200 ml/7 fl oz coconut milk
salt and freshly ground black pepper
4 tbsp freshly chopped coriander
2 spring onions, shredded,
  to garnish
freshly cooked Thai fragrant rice,
  to serve

TASTY TIP

Frying the spices before grinding them helps to release their essential oils. This, in turn, brings out the flavour of the spices, making them much more aromatic.

1 Heat the wok and add the cumin seeds, mustard seeds and coriander seeds. Dry-fry over a low to medium heat for 2 minutes, or until the fragrance becomes stronger and the seeds start to pop. Add the turmeric and leave to cool slightly. Grind the spices in a pestle and mortar or blend to a fine powder in a food processor.

2 Mix the chilli, ginger, garlic and the cream together in a small bowl, add the ground spices and mix. Place the chicken thighs in a shallow dish and spread the spice paste over the thighs.

3 Heat the wok over a high heat, add the oil and when hot, add the onion and stir-fry until golden brown. Add the chicken and spice paste. Cook for 5–6 minutes, stirring occasionally, until evenly coloured. Add the coconut milk and season to taste with salt and pepper. Simmer the chicken for 15–20 minutes, or until the thighs are cooked through, taking care not to allow the mixture to boil. Stir in the chopped coriander and serve immediately with the freshly cooked rice sprinkled with shredded spring onions.

1

2

3

Index